TO

FROM

DATE

God's Priorities
FOR YOUR LIFE

FOR Women

HENDRICKSON
PUBLISHERS

God's Priorities for Your Life for Women

©2006 Hendrickson Publishers, Inc.
P. O. Box 3473
Peabody, MA 01961

ISBN-13: 978-1-59856-124-1
ISBN-10: 1-59856-124-3

Printed in the United States of America

First printing—August 2006

Except for quotations from Scripture, the quoted ideas expressed in this book are not, in all cases, exact quotations, as some have been edited for clarity and brevity. In all cases, the author has attempted to maintain the speaker's original intent. In some cases, quoted material for this book was obtained from secondary sources, primarily print media. While every effort was made to ensure the accuracy of these sources, the accuracy cannot be guaranteed. For additions, deletions, corrections, or clarifications in future editions of this text, please write Hendrickson Publishers, Inc.

Scriptures marked NIV® are from the Holy Bible, New International Version®. Copyright © 1973, 1978, 1984 by International Bible Society. Used by permission of Zondervan Publishing House. All rights reserved.

Scriptures marked NASB are taken from the New American Standard Bible®. © Copyright The Lockman Foundation 1960, 1962, 1963, 1968, 1971, 1972, 1973, 1975, 1977, 1995. Used by permission. (www.Lockman.org).

Scriptures marked NKJV are taken from the New King James Version®. Copyright © 1982 by Thomas Nelson, Inc. Used by permission. All rights reserved.

Scriptures marked NLT are taken from the Holy Bible, New Living Translation, copyright © 1996. Used by permission of Tyndale House Publishers, Inc., Wheaton, Illinois 60189. All rights reserved.

Scriptures marked NCV are quoted from The Holy Bible, New Century Version, copyright © 1987, 1988, 1991 by Word Publishing, Nashville, Tennessee 37214. Used by permission.

Scriptures marked KJV are taken from the King James Version.

Scripture quotations marked MSG are taken from The Message. Copyright © by Eugene H. Peterson 1993, 1994, 1995. Used by permission of NavPress Publishing Group.

Scripture quotations marked ICB are taken from the International Children's Bible, New Century Version © 1986, 1988 by Word Publishing, Nashville, Tennessee 37214. Used by permission.

Scripture quotations marked TLB are taken from The Living Bible copyright © 1971. Used by permission of Tyndale House Publishers, Inc., Wheaton, Illinois 60189. All rights reserved.

Scripture quotations marked Holman CSB are taken from the Holman Christian Standard Bible®, Copyright © 1999, 2000, 2002, 2003 by Holman Bible Publishers. Used by permission. Holman Christian Standard Bible®, Holman CSB®, and HCSB® are federally registered trademarks of Holman Bible Publishers.

Cover Design by Kim Russell / Wahoo Designs
Page Layout by Bart Dawson

God's Priorities

FOR YOUR LIFE

FOR Women

Table of Contents

Introduction

How many decisions do you make in a typical day? When you stop to think about it, you make thousands of choices, usually without too much forethought. Of course, most of these choices are relatively small ones, like what to do at a given moment, or what to say, or how to direct your thoughts. Occasionally, you will face major decisions, like choosing to be a Christian, or choosing a profession, or choosing a spouse. But whatever choices you face, whether they're big, little, or somewhere in between, you can be sure of this: the quality of your choices will make an enormous difference in the quality of your life.

Your choices are shaped by your priorities. Simply put, your priorities determine, to a surprising extent, the quality of the decisions you make and the direction that your life will take. And that's why the ideas in this book are so important.

This book addresses Christian values that can—and should—shape your life. You may find it helpful to read the book from cover to cover, or you may decide to scan the Table of Contents and then turn to chapters that seem particularly important to you. Either way, the ideas on these pages will serve to remind you of God's commandments, God's promises, God's love, and God's Son—all things that are crucially important as you establish priorities for the next stage of your life's journey.

Whose values do you hold most dear: society's values or God's values? When you decide to make God's priorities your priorities, you will receive His abundance and His peace. When you make God a full partner in every aspect of your life, He will lead you along the proper path: His path. When you allow God to direct your steps, He will honor you with spiritual blessings that are simply too numerous to count. So, as you make your next important decision, pause to consider the values that serve as the starting point for that decision. When you do, your decision-making will be vastly improved . . . and so will your life.

Oh, that we might discern the will of God, surrender to His calling, resign the masses of activities, and do a few things well. What a legacy that would be for our children.

Beth Moore

*Let us fix our eyes on Jesus, the author
and perfecter of our faith, who for the joy
set before him endured the cross,
scorning its shame, and sat down
at the right hand of the throne of God.*

Hebrews 12:2 NIV

God's Priorities for Your Life

First pay attention to me, and then relax.
Now you can take it easy—you're in good hands.

Proverbs 1:33 MSG

Has the busy pace of life robbed you of the peace of mind that should rightfully be yours? Has a bloated to-do list left you with little time for yourself and even less time for your loved ones? Are you so busy running from place to place that you scarcely have time to ask yourself where you're running—or why? If so, then you—like so many women who are trying to make ends meet here in the 21st Century—are simply too busy for your own good.

Time is a nonrenewable gift from God. How will you use it? You know from experience that you should invest some time each day in yourself, but finding time to do so is easier said than done. Why? Because so many people are expecting so many things from you!

You live in a noisy world, a world filled with distractions, frustrations, temptations, and obligations. But if you allow the distractions of everyday life to distract you from God's peace, you're doing yourself a big disservice. So here's some good advice: instead of rushing nonstop through the day, slow yourself down long enough to have a few quiet minutes with God.

If you're having trouble prioritizing your day, perhaps you've been trying to organize your life according to your own plans, not God's. A better strategy, of course, is to take your daily obligations and place them in the hands of the One who created you. To do so, you must prioritize your day according to God's commandments, and you must seek His will and His wisdom in all matters. Then, you can face the day with the assurance that the same God who created our universe out of nothingness will help you place first things first in your own life.

As you establish priorities for your day and your life, remember that each new day is a special treasure to be savored and celebrated. As a Christian, you have much to celebrate and much to do. Every day, like every life, is composed of moments. Each moment offers you the potential to seek God's will and to serve His purposes. If you are wise, you will strive to do both.

May you—as a Christian woman who has so much to celebrate—never fail to praise your Creator by rejoicing in this glorious day, and by using it wisely.

PRIORITIES FOR MY LIFE

Make time for God. Even if your day is filled to the brim with obligations and priorities, no priority is greater than our obligation to our Creator. Make sure to give Him the time He deserves, not only on Sundays, but also on every other day of the week.

TIMELESS WISDOM FOR GODLY LIVING

It's sobering to contemplate how much time, effort, sacrifice, compromise, and attention we give to acquiring and increasing our supply of something that is totally insignificant in eternity.

Anne Graham Lotz

Sin is largely a matter of mistaken priorities. Any sin in us that is cherished, hidden, and not confessed will cut the nerve center of our faith.

Catherine Marshall

How important it is for us—young and old—to live as if Jesus would return any day—to set our goals, make our choices, raise our children, and conduct business with the perspective of the imminent return of our Lord.

Gloria Gaither

And I pray this: that your love will keep on growing in knowledge and every kind of discernment, so that you can determine what really matters and can be pure and blameless in the day of Christ.

Philippians 1:9 Holman CSB

The best and most beautiful things in this world cannot be seen or even heard. They must be felt with the heart.

Helen Keller

MORE WORDS FROM GOD'S WORD

The thing you should want most is God's kingdom and doing what God wants. Then all these other things you need will be given to you.

Matthew 6:33 NCV

Let us fix our eyes on Jesus, the author and perfecter of our faith, who for the joy set before him endured the cross, scorning its shame, and sat down at the right hand of the throne of God.

Hebrews 12:2 NIV

You will show me the path of life; in Your presence is fullness of joy; at Your right hand are pleasures forevermore.

Psalm 16:11 NKJV

Whatever you do, do everything for God's glory.

1 Corinthians 10:31 Holman CSB

My Priorities for Life

	Check Your Priority	
High	Med.	Low

I understand the importance of reviewing my priorities frequently . . .

— — —

On my priority list, I put God first and my family second . . .

— — —

I place a high value on doing important tasks first and easy tasks later . . .

— — —

Pleasing God First

Be energetic in your life of salvation, reverent and sensitive before God.
That energy is God's energy, an energy deep within you,
God himself willing and working at what
will give him the most pleasure.

Philippians 2:12-13 MSG

When God made you, He equipped you with an array of talents and abilities that are uniquely yours. It's up to you to discover those talents and to use them, but sometimes the world will encourage you to do otherwise. At times, society will attempt to cubbyhole you, to standardize you, and to make you fit into a particular, preformed mold. Perhaps God has other plans.

Sometimes, because you're an imperfect human being, you may become so wrapped up in meeting society's expectations that you fail to focus on God's expectations. To do so is a mistake of major proportions—don't make it. Instead, seek God's guidance as you focus your energies on becoming the best "you" that you can possibly be. And, when it comes to matters of conscience, seek approval not from your peers, but from your Creator.

Who will you try to please today: God or man? Your primary obligation is not to please imperfect men and women. Your obligation is to strive diligently to meet the expectations of an all-knowing and perfect God. Trust Him always. Love Him always. Praise Him always. And seek to please Him. Always.

Make God's will the focus of your life day by day.
If you seek to please Him and Him alone,
you'll find yourself satisfied with life.

Kay Arthur

*I tried keeping rules and working my head off to please God,
and it didn't work. So I quit being a "law man" so that I could be
God's man. Christ's life showed me how, and enabled me to do it.
I identified myself completely with him. Indeed,
I have been crucified with Christ. My ego is no longer central.*

Galatians 2:19-20 MSG

PRIORITIES FOR MY LIFE

First, focus on your relationship with God. Then, you'll find that
every other relationship and every other aspect of your life will be
more fulfilling.

TIMELESS WISDOM FOR GODLY LIVING

God is not hard to please. He does not expect us to be absolutely perfect. He just expects us to keep moving toward Him and believing in Him, letting Him work with us to bring us into conformity to His will and ways.

Joyce Meyer

If you are receiving your affirmation, love, self worth, joy, strength and acceptance from anywhere but God, He will shake it.

Lisa Bevere

If you really want to please God and intend to be in full agreement with His will, you can't go wrong.

Francis Mary Paul Libermann

By an act of faith, Enoch skipped death completely. "They looked all over and couldn't find him because God had taken him." We know on the basis of reliable testimony that before he was taken "he pleased God."
Hebrews 11:5 MSG

You will get untold flak for prioritizing God's revealed and present will for your life over man's . . . but, boy, is it worth it.

Beth Moore

MORE WORDS FROM GOD'S WORD

Everything that goes into a life of pleasing God has been miraculously given to us by getting to know, personally and intimately, the One who invited us to God. The best invitation we ever received!

2 Peter 1:3 MSG

Our only goal is to please God whether we live here or there, because we must all stand before Christ to be judged.

2 Corinthians 5:9-10 NCV

Do you think I am trying to make people accept me? No, God is the One I am trying to please. Am I trying to please people? If I still wanted to please people, I would not be a servant of Christ.

Galatians 1:10 NCV

My Priorities for Life

I understand that being obedient to God means that I cannot always please other people.

I try to associate with people who, by their actions and their words, will encourage me to become a better person.

I understand that it's more important to be respected than to be liked.

Check Your Priority		
High	Med.	Low
—	—	—
—	—	—
—	—	—

The Life to Which You Are Called

Whatever you do, do all to the glory of God.

1 Corinthians 10:31 NKJV

"What on earth does God intend for me to do with my life?" It's an easy question to ask but, for many of us, a difficult question to answer. Why? Because God's purposes aren't always clear to us. Sometimes, we wander aimlessly in a wilderness of our own making. And sometimes, we struggle mightily against God in an unsuccessful attempt to find success and happiness through our own means, not His.

If you're a woman who sincerely seeks God's guidance, He will give it. But, He will make His revelations known to you in a way and in a time of His choosing, not yours, so be patient. If you prayerfully petition God and work diligently to discern His intentions, He will, in time, lead you to a place of joyful abundance and eternal peace.

Sometimes, God's intentions will be clear to you; other times, God's plan will seem uncertain at best. But even on those difficult days when you are unsure which way to turn, you must never lose sight of these overriding facts: God created you for a reason; He has important work for you to do; and He's waiting patiently for you to do it.

And the next step is up to you.

Only God's chosen task for you will ultimately satisfy.
Do not wait until it is too late to realize the privilege
of serving Him in His chosen position for you.

Beth Moore

We may run, walk, stumble, drive, or fly,
but let us never lose sight of the reason for the journey,
or miss a chance to see a rainbow on the way.

Gloria Gaither

PRIORITIES FOR MY LIFE

God has a wonderful plan for your life. And the time to start looking for that plan—and living it—is now.

TIMELESS WISDOM FOR GODLY LIVING

Victory is the result of Christ's life lived out in the believer. It is important to see that victory, not defeat, is God's purpose for His children.

Corrie ten Boom

How much of our lives are, well, so daily. How often our hours are filled with the mundane, seemingly unimportant things that have to be done, whether at home or work. These very "daily" tasks could become a celebration of praise. "It is through consecration," someone has said, "that drudgery is made divine."

Gigi Graham Tchividjian

How we leave the world is more important than how we enter it.

Janette Oke

You're sons of Light, daughters of Day.
We live under wide open skies and know where we stand.
So let's not sleepwalk through life . . .
1 Thessalonians 5:5-6 MSG

We are most vulnerable to the piercing winds of doubt when we distance ourselves from the mission and fellowship to which Christ has called us.

Joni Eareckson Tada

MORE WORDS FROM GOD'S WORD

We look at this Son and see the God who cannot be seen. We look at this Son and see God's original purpose in everything created.

Colossians 1:15 MSG

To everything there is a season, a time for every purpose under heaven.

Ecclesiastes 3:1 NKJV

There is one thing I always do. Forgetting the past and straining toward what is ahead, I keep trying to reach the goal and get the prize for which God called me . . . .

Philippians 3:13–14 NCV

My Priorities for Life

	Check Your Priority	
High	Med.	Low

I will seek to discover God's unfolding purpose for my life.

— — —

I will consult God on matters great and small.

— — —

I will pray about my plans for the future.

— — —

I will remain open to the opportunities and challenges that God places before me.

— — —

Becoming a Humble Servant

There are different kinds of gifts, but they are all from the same Spirit.
There are different ways to serve but the same Lord to serve.

1 Corinthians 12:4–5 NCV

We live in a world that glorifies power, prestige, fame, and money. But the words of Jesus teach us that the most esteemed men and women are not the widely acclaimed leaders of society; the most esteemed among us are the humble servants of society.

When we experience success, it's easy to puff out our chests and proclaim, "I did that!" But it's wrong. Whatever "it" is, God did it, and He deserves the credit. As Christians, we have been refashioned and saved by Jesus Christ, and that salvation came not because of our own good works but because of God's grace.

Dietrich Bonhoeffer was correct when he observed, "It is very easy to overestimate the importance of our own achievements in comparison with what we owe others." In other words, reality breeds humility.

Are you willing to become a humble servant for Christ? Are you willing to pitch in and make the world a better place, or are you determined to keep all your blessings to yourself? The answer to these questions will determine the quantity and the quality of the service you render to God—and to His children.

Today, you may feel the temptation to take more than you give. You may be tempted to withhold your generosity. Or you may be tempted to build yourself up in the eyes of your friends. Resist these temptations. Instead, serve your friends quietly and without fanfare. Find a need and fill it . . . humbly. Lend a helping hand . . . anonymously. Share a word of kindness . . . with quiet sincerity. As you go about your daily activities, remember that the Savior of all humanity made Himself a servant, and you, as His follower, must do no less.

We can love Jesus in the hungry, the naked, and the destitute who are dying . . . If you love, you will be willing to serve. And you will find Jesus in the distressing disguise of the poor.

Mother Teresa

PRIORITIES FOR MY LIFE

Whatever your age, whatever your circumstances, you can serve: Each stage of life's journey is a glorious opportunity to place yourself in the service of the One who is the Giver of all blessings. As long as you live, you should honor God with your service to others.

TIMELESS WISDOM FOR GODLY LIVING

So many times we say that we can't serve God because we aren't whatever is needed. We're not talented enough or smart enough or whatever. But if you are in covenant with Jesus Christ, He is responsible for covering your weaknesses, for being your strength. He will give you His abilities for your disabilities!

Kay Arthur

In the very place where God has put us, whatever its limitations, whatever kind of work it may be, we may indeed serve the Lord Christ.

Elisabeth Elliot

So prepare your minds for service and have self-control. All your hope should be for the gift of grace that will be yours when Jesus Christ is shown to you.
1 Peter 1:13 NCV

If you want to discover your spiritual gifts, start obeying God. As you serve Him, you will find that He has given you the gifts that are necessary to follow through in obedience.

Anne Graham Lotz

MORE WORDS FROM GOD'S WORD

Therefore, since we receive a kingdom which cannot be shaken, let us show gratitude, by which we may offer to God an acceptable service with reverence and awe....

Hebrews 12:28 NASB

If they serve Him obediently, they will end their days in prosperity and their years in happiness.

Job 36:11 Holman CSB

Whoever serves me must follow me. Then my servant will be with me everywhere I am. My Father will honor anyone who serves me.

John 12:26 NCV

Worship the Lord your God and . . . serve Him only.

Matthew 4:10 Holman CSB

My Priorities for Life

Christ was a humble servant, and I value the importance of following His example.

I believe that greatness in God's kingdom relates to service, not status.

I am proactive in my search to find ways to help others.

Check Your Priority		
High	Med.	Low
—	—	—
—	—	—
—	—	—

Guarding Your Thoughts

And now, dear brothers and sisters, let me say one more thing
as I close this letter. Fix your thoughts on what is true and honorable
and right. Think about things that are pure and lovely and admirable.
Think about things that are excellent and worthy of praise.

Philippians 4:8 NLT

Are you an upbeat believer? Are you a woman whose hopes and dreams are alive and well? Do you regularly have a smile on your face? And then, do you share that smile with family and friends? Hopefully so. After all, when you decided to allow Christ to rule over your heart, you entitled yourself to share in His promise of spiritual abundance and eternal joy. But sometimes, when pessimism and doubt invade your thoughts, you won't feel like celebrating. Why? Because thoughts are intensely powerful things.

Your thoughts have the power to lift you up or drag you down; they have the power to energize you or deplete you, to inspire you to greater accomplishments or to make those accomplishments impossible.

How will you direct your thoughts today? Will you obey the words of Philippians 4:7-8 by dwelling upon those things that are true, noble, reputable, authentic, compelling, and gracious? Or will you allow yourself to be hijacked by the negativity that seems to dominate our troubled world?

Are you fearful, angry, bored, or worried? Are you so preoccupied with the concerns of this day that you fail to thank God for the promise of eternity? Are you confused, bitter, or pessimistic? If so, God wants to have a little talk with you.

God intends that you experience joy and abundance, but He will not force His joy upon you; you must claim it for yourself. It's up to you to celebrate the life that God has given you by focusing your mind upon "whatever is commendable." Today, spend more time thinking about your blessings, and less time fretting about your hardships. Then, take time to thank the Giver of all things good for gifts that are, in truth, far too numerous to count.

As we have by faith said no to sin, so we should by faith
say yes to God and set our minds on things above,
where Christ is seated in the heavenlies.

Vonette Bright

PRIORITIES FOR MY LIFE

Good thoughts create good deeds. Good thoughts lead to good deeds and bad thoughts lead elsewhere. So guard your thoughts accordingly.

TIMELESS WISDOM FOR GODLY LIVING

I am amazed at my own "rut-think" that periodically takes over.

Marilyn Meberg

Preoccupy my thoughts with your praise beginning today.

Joni Eareckson Tada

The things we think are the things that feed our souls. If we think on pure and lovely things, we shall grow pure and lovely like them; and the converse is equally true.

Hannah Whitall Smith

Attitude is the mind's paintbrush; it can color any situation.

Barbara Johnson

Dear friend, guard Clear Thinking and Common Sense with your life; don't for a minute lose sight of them. They'll keep your soul alive and well, they'll keep you fit and attractive.
Proverbs 3:21-22 MSG

Your thoughts are the determining factor as to whose mold you are conformed to. Control your thoughts and you control the direction of your life.

Charles Stanley

MORE WORDS FROM GOD'S WORD

So prepare your minds for service and have self-control.

1 Peter 1:13 NCV

Come near to God, and God will come near to you. You sinners, clean sin out of your lives. You who are trying to follow God and the world at the same time, make your thinking pure.

James 4:8 NCV

Keep your eyes focused on what is right, and look straight ahead to what is good.

Proverbs 4:25 NCV

My Priorities for Life

I understand the importance of directing my thoughts in a proper direction.

I believe that emotions are contagious, so I try to associate with people who are upbeat, optimistic, and encouraging.

I understand that when I dwell on positive thoughts, I feel better about my circumstances and better about myself.

Check Your Priority		
High	Med.	Low
—	—	—
—	—	—
—	—	—

Your Future Is Secure

What a God we have! And how fortunate we are to have him,
this Father of our Master Jesus! Because Jesus was raised from the
dead, we've been given a brand-new life and have everything to live for,
including a future in heaven—and the future starts now!

1 Peter 1:3-4 MSG

Because we are saved by a risen Christ, we can have hope for the future, no matter how troublesome our present circumstances may seem. After all, God has promised that we are His throughout eternity. And, He has told us that we must place our hopes in Him.

Of course, we will face disappointments and failures while we are here on earth, but these are only temporary defeats. Of course, this world can be a place of trials and tribulations, but when we place our trust in the Giver of all things good, we are secure. God has promised us peace, joy, and eternal life. And God keeps His promises today, tomorrow, and forever.

Are you willing to place your future in the hands of a loving and all-knowing God? Do you trust in the ultimate goodness of His plan for your life? Will you face today's challenges with optimism and hope? You should. After all, God created you for a very important purpose: His purpose. And you still have important work to do: His work.

Today, as you live in the present and look to the future, remember that God has a plan for you. Act—and believe—accordingly.

You have a glorious future in Christ!
Live every moment in His power and love.

Vonette Bright

We need to be at peace with our past,
content with our present, and sure about our future,
knowing they are all in God's hands.

Joyce Meyer

PRIORITIES FOR MY LIFE

Anne Graham Lotz writes, "You can look forward with hope, because one day there will be no more separation, no more scars, and no more suffering in My Father's House. It's the home of your dreams!" Now, that's a bright future!

TIMELESS WISDOM FOR GODLY LIVING

Do not limit the limitless God! With Him, face the future unafraid because you are never alone.

Mrs. Charles E. Cowman

For Christians who believe God's promises, the future is actually too bright to comprehend.

Marie T. Freeman

The best we can hope for in this life is a knothole peek at the shining realities ahead. Yet a glimpse is enough. It's enough to convince our hearts that whatever sufferings and sorrows currently assail us aren't worthy of comparison to that which waits over the horizon.

Joni Eareckson Tada

*"I say this because I know what I am planning for you,"
says the Lord. "I have good plans for you, not plans to
hurt you. I will give you hope and a good future."*
Jeremiah 29:11 NCV

Like little children on Christmas Eve, we know that lovely surprises are in the making. We can't see them. We have simply been told, and we believe. Tomorrow we shall see.

Elisabeth Elliot

MORE WORDS FROM GOD'S WORD

Wisdom is pleasing to you. If you find it, you have hope for the future.

Proverbs 24:14 NCV

When troubles come and all these awful things happen to you, in future days you will come back to God, your God, and listen obediently to what he says. God, your God, is above all a compassionate God. In the end he will not abandon you, he won't bring you to ruin, he won't forget the covenant with your ancestors which he swore to them.

Deuteronomy 4:30-31 MSG

Those who trust in the LORD are as secure as Mount Zion; they will not be defeated but will endure forever.

Psalm 125:1 NLT

My Priorities for Life

I try to focus more on future opportunities than on past disappointments.

I believe that building for a better future requires a willingness to get busy and do my work today.

I believe that hope for the future isn't some pie-in-the-sky dream; I believe that hope for the future is simply one aspect of trusting God.

Check Your Priority		
High	Med.	Low
—	—	—
—	—	—
—	—	—

Accepting the Gift of Grace

*But God, who is abundant in mercy, because of His great love
that He had for us, made us alive with the Messiah even though
we were dead in trespasses. By grace you are saved!*

Ephesians 2:4-5 Holman CSB

God's grace is not earned . . . thank goodness! To earn
God's love and His gift of eternal life would be far
beyond the abilities of even the most righteous man or
woman. Thankfully, grace is not an earthly reward for righteous
behavior; it is a blessed spiritual gift which can be accepted by
believers who dedicate themselves to God through Christ. When
we accept Christ into our hearts, we are saved by His grace.

The familiar words of Ephesians 2:8 make God's promise
perfectly clear: It is by grace we have been saved, through faith.
We are saved not because of our good deeds but because of our
faith in Christ.

God's grace is the ultimate gift, and we owe to Him the
ultimate in thanksgiving. Let us praise the Creator for His
priceless gift, and let us share the Good News with all who cross
our paths. We return our Father's love by accepting His grace and
by sharing His message and His love.

Have you thanked God today for blessings that are too numerous to count? Have you offered Him your heartfelt prayers and your wholehearted praise? If not, it's time slow down and offer a prayer of thanksgiving to the One who has given you life on earth and life eternal.

If you are a thoughtful Christian, you will be a thankful Christian. No matter your circumstances, you owe God so much more than you can ever repay, and you owe Him your heartfelt thanks. So thank Him . . . and keep thanking Him, today, tomorrow and forever.

It's clear to me that our gossamer-thin lives are
held together by the glue of God's grace.

Sheila Walsh

PRIORITIES FOR MY LIFE

Remember that His grace is enough . . . God promises that His grace is sufficient for your needs. Believe Him.

TIMELESS WISDOM FOR GODLY LIVING

I have learned that the more we understand how very much
God loves us, and the more we comprehend the grace He has
demonstrated toward us, the more humble we become.

Serita Ann Jakes

When we focus on God, the scene changes. He's in control of our
lives; nothing lies outside the realm of His redemptive grace. Even
when we make mistakes, fail in relationships, or deliberately make
bad choices, God can redeem us.

Penelope J. Stokes

In your greatest weakness, turn to your greatest strength, Jesus,
and hear Him say, "My grace is sufficient for you, for My strength
is made perfect in weakness" (2 Corinthians 12:9, NKJV).

Lisa Whelchel

*Therefore, since we are receiving a kingdom that
cannot be shaken, let us hold on to grace. By it, we may
serve God acceptably, with reverence and awe.*
Hebrews 12:28 Holman CSB

How beautiful it is to learn that grace isn't fragile, and that in the
family of God we can fail and not be a failure.

Gloria Gaither

MORE WORDS FROM GOD'S WORD

For by grace you are saved through faith, and this is not from yourselves; it is God's gift—not from works, so that no one can boast.

Ephesians 2:8-9 Holman CSB

And we have seen and testify that the Father has sent the Son as Savior of the world.

1 John 4:14 NKJV

In Him we have redemption through His blood, the forgiveness of our trespasses, according to the riches of His grace that He lavished on us with all wisdom and understanding.

Ephesians 1:7-8 Holman CSB

My Priorities for Life

I understand that God's gifts to me are priceless treasures.

I appreciate the importance of sharing the transforming message of God's gift of grace.

I trust God's promise that His grace is sufficient for my needs.

Check Your Priority		
High	Med.	Low
—	—	—
—	—	—
—	—	—

Kindness in Action

Be kind to each other, tenderhearted, forgiving one another,
just as God through Christ has forgiven you.

Ephesians 4:32 NLT

In the busyness and confusion of daily life, it is easy to lose focus, and it is easy to become frustrated. We are imperfect human beings struggling to manage our lives as best we can, but we often fall short. When we are distracted or disappointed, we may neglect to share a kind word or a kind deed. This oversight hurts others, but it hurts us most of all.

Kindness is God's commandment. Matthew 25:40 warns, "...Verily I say unto you, Inasmuch as ye have done it unto one of the least of these my brethren, ye have done it unto me" (KJV). When we extend the hand of friendship to those who need it most, God promises His blessings. When we ignore the needs of others—or mistreat them—we risk God's retribution.

Today, slow yourself down and be alert for those who need your smile, your kind words, or your helping hand. Make kindness a high priority and a centerpiece of your dealings with others. They will be blessed, and you will be, too. When you spread a heaping helping of encouragement and hope to the world, you can't help getting a little bit on yourself.

If I am inconsiderate about the comfort of others,
or their feelings, or even their little weaknesses;
if I am careless about their little hurts and miss opportunities
to smooth their way; if I make the sweet running of
household wheels more difficult to accomplish,
then I know nothing of Calvary's love.

Amy Carmichael

*I tell you the truth, whatever you did for one of the least
of these brothers of mine, you did for me.*

Matthew 25:40 NIV

PRIORITIES FOR MY LIFE

You can't just talk about it: In order to be a kind person, you
must do kind things. Thinking about them isn't enough. So get
busy! The day to start being a more generous person is today!

TIMELESS WISDOM FOR GODLY LIVING

Reach out and care for someone who needs the touch of hospitality. The time you spend caring today will be a love gift that will blossom into the fresh joy of God's Spirit in the future.

Emilie Barnes

As much as God loves to hear our worship and adoration, surely he delights all the more in seeing our gratitude translated into simple kindnesses that keep the chain of praise unbroken, alive in others' hearts.

Evelyn Christenson

Showing kindness to others is one of the nicest things we can do for ourselves.

Janette Oke

Carry each other's burdens,
and in this way you will fulfill the law of Christ.
Galatians 6:2 NIV

In a battle of wills, loving kindness is the only weapon that conquers.

Vimalia McClure

MORE WORDS FROM GOD'S WORD

Finally, all of you should be of one mind, full of sympathy toward each other, loving one another with tender hearts and humble minds.

1 Peter 3:8 NLT

And may the Lord make you increase and abound in love to one another and to all.

1 Thessalonians 3:12 NKJV

So, as those who have been chosen of God, holy and beloved, put on a heart of compassion, kindness, humility, gentleness and patience.

Colossians 3:12 NASB

A gentle answer turns away wrath, but a harsh word stirs up anger.

Proverbs 15:1 NIV

My Priorities for Life

I believe that it is important to treat all people with respect and kindness.

I find that when I treat others with respect, I feel better about myself.

When dealing with other people, I believe that it is important to try to "walk in their shoes."

Check Your Priority		
High	Med.	Low
—	—	—
—	—	—
—	—	—

The Wisdom to Be Humble

Clothe yourselves with humility toward one another,
because God resists the proud, but gives grace to the humble.

1 Peter 5:5 Holman CSB

We have heard the phrases on countless occasions: "He's a self-made man," or "she's a self-made woman." In truth, none of us are self-made. We all owe countless debts that we can never repay.

Our first debt, of course, is to our Father in heaven—Who has given us everything—and to His Son Who sacrificed His own life so that we might live eternally. We are also indebted to ancestors, parents, teachers, friends, spouses, family members, coworkers, fellow believers . . . and the list, of course, goes on.

As Christians, we have a profound reason to be humble: We have been refashioned and saved by Jesus Christ, and that salvation came not because of our own good works but because of God's grace. Thus, we are not "self-made," we are "God-made," and "Christ-saved." How, then, can we be boastful? The answer, of course, is that, if we are honest with ourselves and with our God, we simply can't be boastful . . . we must, instead, be eternally grateful and exceedingly humble.

Humility is not, in most cases, a naturally-occurring human trait. Most of us, it seems, are more than willing to stick out our chests and say, "Look at me; I did that!" But in our better moments, in the quiet moments when we search the depths of our own hearts, we know better. Whatever "it" is, God did that, not us.

St. Augustine observed, "If you plan to build a tall house of virtues, you must first lay deep foundations of humility." Are you a believer who genuinely seeks to build your house of virtues on a strong foundation of humility? If so, you are wise and you are blessed. But if you've been laboring under the misconception that you're a "self-made" man or woman, it's time to face facts: your blessings come from God. And He deserves the credit.

I have learned that the more we understand how very much
God loves us, and the more we comprehend the grace
He has demonstrated toward us, the more humble we become.

Serita Ann Jakes

PRIORITIES FOR MY LIFE

Do you value humility above status? If so, God will smile upon your endeavors. But if you value status above humility, you're inviting God's displeasure. In short, humility pleases God; pride does not.

TIMELESS WISDOM FOR GODLY LIVING

Yes, we need to acknowledge our weaknesses, to confess our sins. But if we want to be active, productive participants in the realm of God, we also need to recognize our gifts, to appreciate our strengths, to build on the abilities God has given us. We need to balance humility with confidence.

Penelope Stokes

The gate of heaven is very low; only the humble can enter it.

Elizabeth Ann Seton

If you know who you are in Christ, your personal ego is not an issue.

Beth Moore

Finally, all of you should be of one mind,
full of sympathy toward each other, loving one another
with tender hearts and humble minds.
1 Peter 3:8 NLT

As children observe an attitude and spirit of humility in us, our example will pave the way for them when they must admit to their heavenly Father their own desperate need for guidance and forgiveness.

Annie Chapman

MORE WORDS FROM GOD'S WORD

Therefore humble yourselves under the mighty hand of God, that He may exalt you at the proper time, casting all your anxiety on Him, because He cares for you.

1 Peter 5:6-7 NASB

If My people who are called by My name will humble themselves, and pray and seek My face, and turn from their wicked ways, then I will hear from heaven, and will forgive their sin and heal their land.

2 Chronicles 7:14 NKJV

God has chosen you and made you his holy people. He loves you. So always do these things: Show mercy to others, be kind, humble, gentle, and patient.

Colossians 3:12 NCV

My Priorities for Life

I place a high priority on the need to remain humble before God.

I understand the importance of remaining humble in my dealings with others.

I genuinely seek to give God the honor that He deserves.

Check Your Priority		
High	Med.	Low
—	—	—
—	—	—
—	—	—

The Journey Toward Spiritual Maturity

For this reason we also, since the day we heard it,
do not cease to pray for you, and to ask that you may be filled with
the knowledge of His will in all wisdom and spiritual understanding . . .

Colossians 1:9 NKJV

The path to spiritual maturity unfolds day by day. Each day offers the opportunity to worship God, to ignore God, or to rebel against God. When we worship Him with our prayers, our words, our thoughts, and our actions, we are blessed by the richness of our relationship with the Father. But if we ignore God altogether or intentionally rebel against His commandments, we rob ourselves of His blessings.

If we study God's Word, if we obey His commandments, and if we live in the center of His will, we will not be "stagnant" believers; we will, instead, be growing Christians . . . and that's exactly what God wants for our lives.

Many of life's most important lessons are painful to learn, but spiritual growth need not take place only in times of adversity. We must seek to grow in our knowledge and love of the Lord in every season of life. Thankfully, God always stands at the door; whenever we are ready to reach out to Him, He will answer.

In those quiet moments when we open our hearts to the Father, the One who made us keeps remaking us. He gives us direction, perspective, wisdom, and courage. And, the appropriate moment to accept those spiritual gifts is always the present one.

Are you as mature as you're ever going to be? Hopefully not! When it comes to your faith, God doesn't intend for you to become "fully grown," at least not in this lifetime. In fact, God still has important lessons that He intends to teach you. So ask yourself this: what lesson is God trying to teach me today? And then go about the business of learning it.

The whole idea of belonging to Christ is to look less and less like we used to and more and more like Him.

Angela Thomas

PRIORITIES FOR MY LIFE

Change Is Inevitable; Growth Is Not: The world keeps changing, and so, hopefully, do we. We are mightily tempted to remain stagnant (we perceive that it's safer "here" than "there"). But God has bigger plans for us. He intends that we continue to mature throughout every stage of life. Toward that end, God comes to our doorsteps with countless opportunities to learn and to grow. And He knocks. Our challenge, of course, is to open the door.

TIMELESS WISDOM FOR GODLY LIVING

As I have continued to grow in my Christian maturity, I have discovered that the Holy Spirit does not let me get by with anything.

Anne Graham Lotz

Grace meets you where you are, but it doesn't leave you where it found you.

Anne Lamott

Recently I've been learning that life comes down to this: God is in everything. Regardless of what difficulties I am experiencing at the moment, or what things aren't as I would like them to be, I look at the circumstances and say, "Lord, what are you trying to teach me?"

Catherine Marshall

So let us stop going over the basics of Christianity again and again. Let us go on instead and become mature in our understanding.
Hebrews 6:1 NLT

If I long to improve my brother, the first step toward doing so is to improve myself.

Christina Rossetti

MORE WORDS FROM GOD'S WORD

Run away from infantile indulgence. Run after mature righteousness—faith, love, peace—joining those who are in honest and serious prayer before God.

2 Timothy 2:22 MSG

Know the love of Christ which surpasses knowledge, that you may be filled up to all the fullness of God.

Ephesians 3:19 NASB

For You, O God, have tested us; You have refined us as silver is refined. You brought us into the net; You laid affliction on our backs. You have caused men to ride over our heads; we went through fire and through water; but You brought us out to rich fulfillment.

Psalm 66:10–12 NKJV

My Priorities for Life

| | Check Your Priority | |
High	Med.	Low
—	—	—

I understand the value of spiritual growth.

| — | — | — |

I believe that spiritual maturity is a journey, not a destination.

| — | — | — |

I believe that regular, consistent study of God's Word ensures that I will continue to grow as a Christian.

Quick to Forgive

Be even-tempered, content with second place, quick to forgive an offense.
Forgive as quickly and completely as the Master forgave you.
And regardless of what else you put on, wear love. It's your basic,
all-purpose garment. Never be without it.

Colossians 3:13-14 MSG

Even the most mild-mannered women will, on occasion, have reason to become angry with the inevitable shortcomings of family members and friends. But wise women are quick to forgive others, just as God has forgiven them.

The commandment to forgive others is clearly a part of God's Word, but oh how difficult a commandment it can be to follow. Because we are imperfect beings, we are quick to anger, quick to blame, slow to forgive, and even slower to forget. No matter. Even when forgiveness is difficult, God's instructions are straightforward: As Christians who have received the gift of forgiveness, we must now share that gift with others.

If, in your heart, you hold bitterness against even a single person, forgive. If there exists even one person, alive or dead, whom you have not forgiven, follow God's commandment and His will for your life: forgive. If you are embittered against yourself for some past mistake or shortcoming, forgive. Then, to the best of your abilities, forget, and move on. Bitterness and regret are not part of God's plan for your life. Forgiveness is. And once you've forgiven others, you can then turn your thoughts to a far more pleasant subject: the incredibly bright future that God has promised.

I believe that forgiveness can become a continuing cycle:
because God forgives us, we're to forgive others;
because we forgive others, God forgives us.
Scripture presents both parts of the cycle.

Shirley Dobson

God expects us to forgive others as He has forgiven us;
we are to follow His example by having a forgiving heart.

Vonette Bright

PRIORITIES FOR MY LIFE

Forgive . . . and keep forgiving! Sometimes, you may forgive someone once and then, at a later time, become angry at the very same person again. If so, you must forgive that person again and again . . . until it sticks.

TIMELESS WISDOM FOR GODLY LIVING

Forgiveness is actually the best revenge because it not only sets us free from the person we forgive, but it frees us to move into all that God has in store for us.

Stormie Omartian

When God forgives, He forgets. He buries our sins in the sea and puts a sign on the shore saying, "No Fishing Allowed."

Corrie ten Boom

Redeemed, how I love to proclaim it! Redeemed by the blood of the Lamb; Redeemed through His infinite mercy, His child, and forever, I am.

Fanny Crosby

Hatred stirs up trouble, but love forgives all wrongs.
Proverbs 10:12 NCV

There is nothing, absolutely nothing, that God will not forgive. You cannot "out-sin" His forgiveness. You cannot "out-sin" the love of God.

Kathy Troccoli

MORE WORDS FROM GOD'S WORD

Our Father is kind; you be kind. "Don't pick on people, jump on their failures, criticize their faults—unless, of course, you want the same treatment. Don't condemn those who are down; that hardness can boomerang. Be easy on people; you'll find life a lot easier.

Luke 6:36-37 MSG

Be gentle with one another, sensitive. Forgive one another as quickly and thoroughly as God in Christ forgave you.

Ephesians 4:32 MSG

Whenever you stand praying, forgive, if you have anything against anyone, so that your Father in heaven will also forgive you your transgressions.

Mark 11:25 NASB

My Priorities for Life

For me, forgiveness is not optional; it is a commandment from God.

I consider forgiveness to be a way of liberating myself from the chains of the past.

Forgiving other people is one way of strengthening my relationship with God.

Check Your Priority		
High	Med.	Low
—	—	—
—	—	—
—	—	—

What Kind of Example?

You should be an example to the believers in speech,
in conduct, in love, in faith, in purity.

1 Timothy 4:12 Holman CSB

Whether we like it or not, all of us are role models. Our friends and family members watch our actions and, as followers of Christ, we are obliged to act accordingly.

What kind of example are you? Are you the kind of woman whose life serves as a genuine example of righteousness? Are you a woman whose behavior serves as a positive role model for young people? Are you the kind of woman whose actions, day in and day out, are based upon kindness, faithfulness, and a love for the Lord? If so, you are not only blessed by God, you are also a powerful force for good in a world that desperately needs positive influences such as yours.

Corrie ten Boom advised, "Don't worry about what you do not understand. Worry about what you do understand in the Bible but do not live by." And that's sound advice because our families and friends are watching . . . and so, for that matter, is God.

In serving we uncover the greatest fulfillment within
and become a stellar example of a woman
who knows and loves Jesus.

Vonette Bright

Let us preach you, Dear Jesus, without preaching,
not by words but by our example, by the casting force,
the sympathetic influence of what we do,
the evident fullness of the love our hearts bear to you.
Amen.

Mother Teresa

PRIORITIES FOR MY LIFE

Live according to the principles you teach. The sermons you live
are far more important than the sermons you preach.

TIMELESS WISDOM FOR GODLY LIVING

Your life is destined to be an example. The only question is "what kind?"

Marie T. Freeman

The religion of Jesus Christ has an ethical as well as a doctrinal side.

Lottie Moon

"I read about it in the Bible" is true and good. Yet, "I have seen him with the eyes of my heart" is often more convincing. And convicting.

Liz Curtis Higgs

We have around us many people whose lives tell us what faith means. So let us run the race that is before us and never give up. We should remove from our lives anything that would get in the way and the sin that so easily holds us back.

Hebrews 12:1 NCV

We are to leave an impression on all those we meet that communicates whose we are and what kingdom we represent.

Lisa Bevere

MORE WORDS FROM GOD'S WORD

In every way be an example of doing good deeds. When you teach, do it with honesty and seriousness.

Titus 2:7 NCV

In everything you do, stay away from complaining and arguing, so that no one can speak a word of blame against you. You are to live clean, innocent lives as children of God in a dark world full of crooked and perverse people. Let your lives shine brightly before them.

Philippians 2:14-15 NLT

You are the light that gives light to the world. In the same way, you should be a light for other people. Live so that they will see the good things you do and will praise your Father in heaven.

Matthew 5:14, 16 NCV

My Priorities for Life

	Check Your Priority	
High	Med.	Low

I value the importance of setting a good example.

— — —

I understand that my behavior speaks volumes about my relationship with God.

— — —

I understand that I am a role model to my family and friends, and I behave accordingly.

— — —

Loving God . . . With All Your Heart

We love Him because He first loved us.

1 John 4:19 NKJV

Do you value you relationship with God . . . and do you tell Him so many times each day? Hopefully so. But if you find yourself overwhelmed by the demands of everyday life, you may find yourself scurrying from place to place with scarcely a spare moment to think about your relationship with the Creator. If so, you're simply too busy for your own good.

God calls each of us to worship Him, to obey His commandments, and to accept His Son as our Savior. When we do, God blesses us in ways that we can scarcely understand. But, when we allow the demands of the day to interfere with our communications with the Father, we unintentionally distance ourselves from our greatest source of abundance and peace.

C. S. Lewis observed, "A person's spiritual health is exactly proportional to his love for God." If we are to enjoy the spiritual health that God intends for us, we must praise Him, we must love Him, and we must obey Him.

When we worship God faithfully and obediently, we invite His love into our hearts. When we truly worship God, we allow

Him to rule over our days and our lives. In turn, we grow to love God even more deeply as we sense His love for us.

St. Augustine wrote, "I love you, Lord, not doubtingly, but with absolute certainty. Your Word beat upon my heart until I fell in love with you, and now the universe and everything in it tells me to love you."

Today, open your heart to the Father. Make yourself His dutiful servant as you follow in the footsteps of His only begotten Son. And let your obedience to the Father be a fitting response to His never-ending love.

To love God is to love His will.

Elisabeth Elliot

PRIORITIES FOR MY LIFE

Express yourself. If you sincerely love God, don't be bashful to tell Him so. And while you're at it, don't be bashful to tell other people about your feelings. If you love God, say so!

TIMELESS WISDOM FOR GODLY LIVING

Joy is a by-product not of happy circumstances, education or talent, but of a healthy relationship with God and a determination to love Him no matter what.

Barbara Johnson

A wholehearted love for God looks to Him through His Word and prayer, always watching and waiting, ever ready to do all that He says, prepared to act on His expressed desires.

Elizabeth George

Delighting thyself in the Lord is the sudden realization that He has become the desire of your heart.

Beth Moore

By this we know that we love the children of God, when we love God and keep His commandments.
1 John 5:2 NKJV

When an honest soul can get still before the living Christ, we can still hear Him say simply and clearly, "Love the Lord your God with all your heart and with all your soul and with all your mind . . . and love one another as I have loved you."

Gloria Gaither

MORE WORDS FROM GOD'S WORD

I will sing of the LORD's great love forever; with my mouth I will make your faithfulness known through all generations.

Psalm 89:1 NIV

And we know that in all things God works for the good of those who love him, who have been called according to his purpose.

Romans 8:28 NIV

Jesus replied, "'Love the Lord your God with all your heart and with all your soul and with all your mind.' This is the first and greatest commandment. And the second is like it: 'Love your neighbor as yourself.' All the Law and the Prophets hang on these two commandments."

Matthew 22:37-40 NIV

My Priorities for Life

	Check Your Priority	
High	Med.	Low

In response to His great love for me, I love God.

—   —   —

I understand that obedience is one way of expressing my love for God.

—   —   —

I believe that loving God is more than a temporary feeling. I understand that I must love God with my heart, my soul, and my mind.

—   —   —

Critics Beware

Don't speak evil against each other, my dear brothers and sisters.
If you criticize each other and condemn each other, then you are
criticizing and condemning God's law. But you are not a judge who
can decide whether the law is right or wrong. Your job is to obey it.

James 4:11 NLT

From experience, we know that it is easier to criticize than to correct. And we know that it is easier to find faults than solutions. Yet the urge to criticize others remains a powerful temptation for most of us.

In verse 11, James issues a clear warning: against criticizing others. Undoubtedly, James understood the paralyzing power of chronic negativity, and so should we. Our task, as obedient believers, is to break the twin habits of negative thinking and critical speech.

Negativity is highly contagious: we give it to others who, in turn, give it back to us. This cycle can be broken by positive thoughts, heartfelt prayers, and encouraging words. As thoughtful servants of a loving God, we can use the transforming power of Christ's love to break the chains of negativity. And we should.

The business of finding fault is very easy,
and that of doing better is very difficult.

Francis de Sales

*Those people are on a dark spiral downward. But if you think
that leaves you on the high ground where you can point your finger at
others, think again. Every time you criticize someone, you condemn
yourself. It takes one to know one. Judgmental criticism of others
is a well-known way of escaping detection in your own crimes and
misdemeanors. But God isn't so easily diverted. He sees right through
all such smoke screens and holds you to what you've done.*

Romans 2:1-2 MSG

PRIORITIES FOR MY LIFE

We human beings are hard-wired with the tendency to blame,
to judge, to gossip, and to criticize. And if some of those words
describe your behavior, pray about it . . . and keep praying about
it . . . until God helps you correct those bad habits.

TIMELESS WISDOM FOR GODLY LIVING

If I long to improve my brother, the first step toward doing so is to improve myself.

Christina Rossetti

It takes less sense to criticize than to do anything else. There are a great many critics in the asylum.

Sam Jones

Being a father is teaching me that when I am criticized, injured, or afraid, there is a Father who is ready to comfort me.

Max Lucado

Jesus draws near to those who are afflicted and persecuted and criticized and ostracized.

Anne Graham Lotz

> *So in everything, do to others what you would have them do to you, for this sums up the Law and the Prophets.*
> Matthew 7:12 NIV

Discouraged people don't need critics. They hurt enough already. They don't need more guilt or piled-on distress. They need encouragement. They need a refuge, a willing, caring, available someone.

Charles Swindoll

MORE WORDS FROM GOD'S WORD

A man who lacks judgment derides his neighbor, but a man of understanding holds his tongue.

Proverbs 11:12 NIV

So let's agree to use all our energy in getting along with each other. Help others with encouraging words; don't drag them down by finding fault.

Romans 14:19-20 MSG

Our Father is kind; you be kind. "Don't pick on people, jump on their failures, criticize their faults—unless, of course, you want the same treatment. Don't condemn those who are down; that hardness can boomerang. Be easy on people; you'll find life a lot easier.

Luke 6:36-37 MSG

My Priorities for Life

I understand that the Bible warns me not to be judgmental of others, and I take that warning seriously.

I understand that my ability to judge others requires a divine insight that I simply don't have.

When I catch myself being overly judgmental, I try to stop myself and interrupt my critical thoughts before I become angry.

Check Your Priority		
High	Med.	Low
—	—	—
—	—	—
—	—	—

Beyond Busyness

Don't burn out; keep yourselves fueled and aflame.
Be alert servants of the Master, cheerfully expectant.
Don't quit in hard times; pray all the harder.

Romans 12:11-12 MSG

The busy pace of life can rob you of the peace that might otherwise be yours through Jesus Christ. Sometimes, you are simply too busy for your own good. Jesus offers you a peace that passes human understanding, but He won't force His peace upon you; in order to experience it, you must slow down long enough to sense His presence and His love.

As a busy person, you may have difficulty investing large blocks of time in much-needed thought and self-reflection. If so, it may be time to reorder your priorities and your values.

God has big plans for you. Discovering those plans will require trial and error, meditation and prayer, faith and perseverance. The moments that you spend with God will help you gather your thoughts and plan for the future. And the time that you spend discussing your dreams with friends and mentors can be invaluable. But, no one can force you to carve out time for life's meaningful moments; it's up to you.

Each waking moment holds the potential to think a creative thought or offer a heartfelt prayer. So even if you're a person with too many demands and too few hours in which to meet them, don't panic. Instead, be comforted in the knowledge that when you sincerely seek to discover God's purpose for your life, He will respond in marvelous and surprising ways. Remember: this is the day that He has made and that He has filled it with countless opportunities to love, to serve, and to seek His guidance. Seize those opportunities today, and keep seizing them every day that you live.

Getting things accomplished isn't nearly
as important as taking time for love.

Janette Oke

PRIORITIES FOR MY LIFE

Feeling overwhelmed? Perhaps you're not doing a very good job of setting priorities—or perhaps you're allowing other people to set your priorities for you.

TIMELESS WISDOM FOR GODLY LIVING

Frustration is not the will of God. There is time to do anything and everything that God wants us to do.

Elisabeth Elliot

In our tense, uptight society where folks are rushing to make appointments they have already missed, a good laugh can be a refreshing as a cup of cold water in the desert.

Barbara Johnson

When a church member gets overactive and public worship is neglected, his or her relationship with God will be damaged.

Anne Ortlund

Careful planning puts you ahead in the long run; hurry and scurry puts you further behind.
Proverbs 21:5 MSG

How much of our lives are, well, so daily. How often our hours are filled with the mundane, seemingly unimportant things that have to be done, whether at home or work. These very "daily" tasks could become a celebration of praise. "It is through consecration," someone has said, "that drudgery is made divine."

Gigi Graham Tchividjian

MORE WORDS FROM GOD'S WORD

You can't go wrong when you love others. When you add up everything in the law code, the sum total is love. But make sure that you don't get so absorbed and exhausted in taking care of all your day-by-day obligations that you lose track of the time and doze off, oblivious to God.

Romans 13:10-11 MSG

But Martha was pulled away by all she had to do in the kitchen. Later, she stepped in, interrupting them. "Master, don't you care that my sister has abandoned the kitchen to me? Tell her to lend me a hand." The Master said, "Martha, dear Martha, you're fussing far too much and getting yourself worked up over nothing. One thing only is essential, and Mary has chosen it—it's the main course, and won't be taken from her."

Luke 10:40-42 MSG

My Priorities for Life

	Check Your Priority	
High	Med.	Low

I understand the danger of being too busy.

— — —

After I have established priorities for the coming day, I value the importance of doing first things first.

— — —

Because I understand that I cannot do everything, I understand the importance of saying no when it's appropriate to do so.

— — —

Richly Blessed

Everything created by God is good, and nothing is to be rejected,
if it is received with gratitude;
for it is sanctified by means of the word of God and prayer.

1 Timothy 4:4-5 NASB

As believers who have been touched by God's grace, we are blessed beyond measure. God sent His only Son to die for our sins. And, God has given us the priceless gifts of eternal love and eternal life. We, in turn, are instructed to approach our Heavenly Father with reverence and thanksgiving. But, as busy people caught up in the inevitable demands of everyday life, we sometimes fail to pause and thank our Creator for the countless blessings that He has bestowed upon us.

Sometimes life is complicated; sometimes life is frustrating; and sometimes life is downright exhausting. When the demands of life leave us rushing from place to place with scarcely a moment to spare, we may fail to pause and thank our Creator for His gifts. Yet, whenever we neglect to give proper thanks to the Giver of all things good, we suffer because of our misplaced priorities.

The words of 1 Thessalonians 5:18 remind us to give thanks in every circumstance of life: "In everything give thanks; for this is the will of God in Christ Jesus for you" (NKJV). But sometimes, when our hearts are troubled and our lives seem to be spinning out of control, we don't feel like thanking anybody, including our Father in heaven. Yet God's Word is clear: In all circumstances, our Creator offers us His love, His strength, and His Grace. And in all circumstances, we must thank Him.

Thoughtful believers (like you) see the need to praise God with sincerity, with humility, and with consistency. So whatever your circumstances—even if you are overworked, over-committed, and overstressed—slow down and express your thanks to the Creator. When you do, you'll discover that your expressions of gratitude will enrich your own life as well as the lives of your loved ones.

Thanksgiving should become a habit, a regular part of your daily routine. After all, God has blessed you beyond measure, and you owe Him everything, including your eternal gratitude . . . starting now.

We become happy, spiritually prosperous people
not because we receive what we want,
but because we appreciate what we have.

Penelope Stokes

PRIORITIES FOR MY LIFE

Whose values? You can have the values that the world holds dear, or you can have the values that God holds dear, but you can't have both. The decision is yours . . . and so are the consequences.

TIMELESS WISDOM FOR GODLY LIVING

Gratitude unlocks the fullness of life. It turns what we have into enough, and more. It turns denial into acceptance, chaos to order, confusion to clarity. It can turn a meal into a feast, a house into a home, a stranger into a friend. Gratitude makes sense of our past, brings peace for today, and creates a vision for tomorrow.

Melody Beattie

A sense of gratitude for God's presence in our lives will help open our eyes to what he has done in the past and what he will do in the future.

Emilie Barnes

As you therefore have received Christ Jesus the Lord, so walk in Him, having been firmly rooted and now being built up in Him and established in your faith, just as you were instructed, and overflowing with gratitude.

Colossians 2:6-7 NASB

Think of the blessings we so easily take for granted: Life itself; preservation from danger; every bit of health we enjoy; every hour of liberty; the ability to see, to hear, to speak, to think, and to imagine all this comes from the hand of God.

Billy Graham

MORE WORDS FROM GOD'S WORD

Let the message about the Messiah dwell richly among you, teaching and admonishing one another in all wisdom, and singing psalms, hymns, and spiritual songs, with gratitude in your hearts to God.

Colossians 3:16 Holman CSB

Therefore, since we receive a kingdom which cannot be shaken, let us show gratitude, by which we may offer to God an acceptable service with reverence and awe . . . .

Hebrews 12:28 NASB

It is good to give thanks to the Lord, to sing praises to the Most High. It is good to proclaim your unfailing love in the morning, your faithfulness in the evening.

Psalm 92:1-2 NLT

My Priorities for Life

I understand the importance of thanking God for His gifts.

I will strive to search for opportunities, not problems.

I will praise God for His perfect plan even when I don't understand that plan.

Check Your Priority		
High	Med.	Low
—	—	—
—	—	—
—	—	—

Stewardship of Your Time

Dear friends, don't let this one thing escape you:
with the Lord one day is like 1,000 years,
and 1,000 years like one day.

2 Peter 3:8 Holman CSB

Do you place a high value on your time? Hopefully you do. After all, time is a precious, nonrenewable gift from God. But sometimes, amid the complications of daily life, you will be sorely tempted to squander the time that God has given you. Why? Because you live in a society filled to the brim with powerful temptations and countless distractions, all of which take time.

An important element of your stewardship to God is the way that you choose to spend the time He has entrusted to you. Each waking moment holds the potential to help a friend, or aid a stranger, to say a kind word, or think a noble thought, or offer a heartfelt prayer. Your challenge, as a believer, is to value your time, to use it judiciously, and to use it in ways that honor your Heavenly Father.

As you establish priorities for your day and your life, remember that each new day is a special treasure to be savored and celebrated. As a Christian, you have much to celebrate and much to do. It's up to you, and you alone, to honor God for the gift of time by using that gift wisely. Every day, like every life, is composed of moments. Each moment of your life holds within it the potential to seek God's will and to serve His purposes. If you are wise, you will strive to do both.

How will you invest your time today? Will you savor the moments of your life, or will you squander them? Will you use your time as an instrument of God's will, or will you allow commonplace distractions to rule your day and your life?

The gift of time is indeed a gift from God. Treat it as if it were a precious, fleeting, one-of-a-kind treasure. Because it is.

I've finally realized that if something has no significant value, it doesn't deserve my time. Life is not a dress rehearsal, and I'll never get this day again.

Sheri Rose Shepherd

PRIORITIES FOR MY LIFE

If you don't value your time . . . neither will anybody else.

TIMELESS WISDOM FOR GODLY LIVING

Does God care about all the responsibilities we have to juggle in our daily lives? Of course. But he cares more that our lives demonstrate balance, the ability to discern what is essential and give ourselves fully to it.

Penelope Stokes

The work of God is appointed. There is always enough time to do the will of God.

Elisabeth Elliot

God has a present will for your life. It is neither chaotic nor utterly exhausting. In the midst of many good choices vying for your time, He will give you the discernment to recognize what is best.

Beth Moore

Life's unfolding stops for no one.

Kathy Troccoli

*There is an occasion for everything,
and a time for every activity under heaven.*
Ecclesiastes 3:1 Holman CSB

The more time you give to something, the more you reveal its importance and value to you.

Rick Warren

MORE WORDS FROM GOD'S WORD

Lord, tell me when the end will come and how long I will live. Let me know how long I have. You have given me only a short life; my lifetime is like nothing to you. Everyone's life is only a breath.

Psalm 39:4-5 NCV

We can't afford to waste a minute, must not squander these precious daylight hours in frivolity and indulgence, in sleeping around and dissipation, in bickering and grabbing everything in sight. Get out of bed and get dressed! Don't loiter and linger, waiting until the very last minute. Dress yourselves in Christ, and be up and about!

Romans 13:13-14 MSG

And the world with its lust is passing away, but the one who does God's will remains forever.

1 John 2:17 Holman CSB

My Priorities for Life

I understand the importance of setting priorities.

I believe that time is a nonrenewable resource that can be invested or squandered.

I understand that one form of stewardship is the stewardship of my time.

Check Your Priority		
High	Med.	Low
—	—	—
—	—	—
—	—	—

Earthly Stress, Heavenly Peace

LORD, help! they cried in their trouble,
and he saved them from their distress.

Psalm 107:13 NLT

Stressful days are an inevitable fact of modern life. And how do we best cope with the challenges of our demanding, 21st-century world? By turning our days and our lives over to God. Elisabeth Elliot writes, "If my life is surrendered to God, all is well. Let me not grab it back, as though it were in peril in His hand but would be safer in mine!" Yet even the most devout Christian woman may, at times, seek to grab the reins of her life and proclaim, "I'm in charge!" To do so is foolish, prideful, and stressful.

When we seek to impose our own wills upon the world—or upon other people—we invite stress into our lives . . . needlessly. But, when we turn our lives and our hearts over to God—when we accept His will instead of seeking vainly to impose our own—we discover the inner peace that can be ours through Him.

Do you feel overwhelmed by the stresses of daily life? Turn your concerns and your prayers over to God. Trust Him. Trust Him completely. Trust Him today. Trust Him always. When it comes to the inevitable challenges of this day, hand them over to God completely and without reservation. He knows your needs and will meet those needs in His own way and in His own time if you let Him.

Don't be overwhelmed . . .
take it one day and one prayer at a time.

Stormie Omartian

Be strong and brave, and do the work.
Don't be afraid or discouraged, because the Lord God, my God,
is with you. He will not fail you or leave you.

1 Chronicles 28:20 NCV

PRIORITIES FOR MY LIFE

If you sincerely want to reduce the stress in your life . . . pray for God's guidance and ask for God's help.

TIMELESS WISDOM FOR GODLY LIVING

God knows what each of us is dealing with. He knows our pressures. He knows our conflicts. And, He has made a provision for each and every one of them. That provision is Himself in the person of the Holy Spirit, dwelling in us and empowering us to respond rightly.

Kay Arthur

The next time the demands of the day leave you stressed, remember the peace of God that comes through Christ Jesus. Open your heart to Him, and He will give you a peace that endures forever: His peace.

Jim Gallery

You have allowed me to suffer much hardship, but you will restore me to life again and lift me up from the depths of the earth. You will restore me to even greater honor and comfort me once again.
Psalm 71:20-21 NLT

When frustrations develop into problems that stress you out, the best way to cope is to stop, catch your breath, and do something for yourself, not out of selfishness, but out of wisdom.

Barbara Johnson

MORE WORDS FROM GOD'S WORD

When my heart is overwhelmed: lead me to the rock that is higher than I.

Psalm 61:2 KJV

God, who comforts the downcast, comforted us . . . .

2 Corinthians 7:6 NIV

For You, O God, have tested us; You have refined us as silver is refined.
You brought us into the net; You laid affliction on our backs. You have
caused men to ride over our heads; we went through fire and through
water; but You brought us out to rich fulfillment.

Psalm 66:10–12 NKJV

My Priorities for Life

	Check Your Priority	
High	Med.	Low

I understand the importance of managing the
inevitable stresses of everyday living.

— — —

I understand the need to pray as if everything
depended upon God and work as if everything
depended upon me.

— — —

Physically, I manage stress through sensible exercise
and sensible rest.

— — —

Spiritually, I deal with stress by letting God handle
my problems.

— — —

The Rule That Is Golden

Just as you want others to do for you, do the same for them.

Luke 6:31 Holman CSB

John Wesley's advice was straightforward: "Do all the good you can. By all the means you can. In all the ways you can. In all the places you can. At all the times you can. To all the people you can. As long as you can." One way to do all the good you can is to spread kindness wherever you go.

Sometimes, when we feel happy or generous, we find it easy to be kind. Other times, when we are discouraged or tired, we can scarcely summon the energy to utter a single kind word. But, God's commandment is clear: He intends that we make the conscious choice to treat others with kindness and respect, no matter our circumstances, no matter our emotions.

St. Teresa of Avila observed, "There are only two duties required of us—the love of God and the love of our neighbor, and the surest sign of discovering whether we observe these duties is the love of our neighbor." Her words remind us that we honor God by serving our friends and neighbors with kind words, heartfelt prayers, and helping hands. If we sincerely desire to

follow in the footsteps of God's Son, we must make kind.
generosity the hallmark of our dealings with others.

Do you look for opportunities to share God's love with you
family and friends? Hopefully you do. After all, your Heavenly
Father has blessed you in countless ways, and He has instructed
you to share your blessings with the world. So today, look for
opportunities to spread kindness wherever you go. God deserves
no less, and neither, for that matter, do your loved ones.

The Golden Rule starts at home,
but it should never stop there.

Marie T. Freeman

PRIORITIES FOR MY LIFE

Kind words cost nothing, but when they're spoken at the right
time, they can be priceless.

WISDOM FOR GODLY LIVING

beautiful compensations of life that no one
help another without helping herself.

Barbara Johnson

Here lies the tremendous mystery—that God should be all-powerful, yet refuse to coerce. He summons us to cooperation. We are honored in being given the opportunity to participate in His good deeds. Remember how He asked for help in performing His miracles: Fill the water pots, stretch out your hand, distribute the loaves.

Elisabeth Elliot

Let us not become weary in doing good,
for at the proper time we will reap
a harvest if we do not give up.
Galatians 6:9 NIV

Trying to do good to people without God's help is no easier than making the sun shine at midnight. You discover that you've got to abandon all your own preferences, your own bright ideas, and guide souls along the road the Lord has marked out for them. You mustn't coerce them into some path of your own choosing.

St. Thérèse of Lisieux

MORE WORDS FROM GOD'S WORD

Each of you should look not only to your own interests, but also to the interest of others.

Philippians 2:4 NIV

Carry each other's burdens, and in this way you will fulfill the law of Christ.

Galatians 6:2 NIV

See that no one renders evil for evil to anyone, but always pursue what is good both for yourselves and for all.

1 Thessalonians 5:15 NKJV

In everything set them an example by doing what is good.

Titus 2:7 NIV

My Priorities for Life

As a Christian, I feel that it is my obligation to be kind to others.

In all my decisions I seek to apply the Golden Rule.

When I extend the hand of kindness to others, I feel that it is important for me to avoid public acclaim.

Check Your Priority		
High	Med.	Low
—	—	—
—	—	—
—	—	—

A High Priority on Prayer

This section is a good reminder.

> *Rejoice evermore. Pray without ceasing.*
> *In every thing give thanks: for this is the will of God*
> *in Christ Jesus concerning you.*
>
> 1 Thessalonians 5:16-18 KJV

Does prayer play an important role in your life? Is prayer an integral part of your daily routine or is it a hit-or-miss activity? Do you "pray without ceasing," or is your prayer life an afterthought? If you genuinely wish to receive the abundance that Christ promises in John 10:10, then you must pray constantly . . . and you must never underestimate the power of prayer.

As you contemplate the quality of your prayer life, here are a few things to consider:

1. God hears our prayers and answers them (Jeremiah 29:11-12).
2. God promises that the prayers of righteous men and women can accomplish great things (James 5:16).
3. God invites us to be still and to feel His presence (Psalm 46:10).

So pray. Start praying in the early morning and keep praying until you fall off to sleep at night. Pray about matters great and small; and be watchful for the answers that God most assuredly sends your way.

Daily prayer and meditation is a matter of will and habit. When you organize your day to include quiet moments with God, you'll soon discover that no time is more precious than the silent moments you spend with Him.

The quality of your spiritual life will be in direct proportion to the quality of your prayer life. So do yourself a favor: instead of turning things over in your mind, turn them over to God in prayer. Instead of worrying about your next decision, ask God to lead the way. Don't limit your prayers to meals or to bedtime. Pray constantly because God is listening—and He wants to hear from you. And without question, you need to hear from Him.

Jesus likes us to vocalize our needs.

Liz Curtis Higgs

PRIORITIES FOR MY LIFE

Prayer strengthens your relationship with God. Beth Moore writes, "Prayer keeps us in constant communion with God, which is the goal of our entire believing lives." It's up to each of us to live—and pray—accordingly.

TIMELESS WISDOM FOR GODLY LIVING

The manifold rewards of a serious, consistent prayer life demonstrate clearly that time with our Lord should be our first priority.

Shirley Dobson

When we feel like the prey, a victim of evil pursuit, it's time for us to pray and take action against our predator.

Serita Ann Jakes

The center of power is not to be found in summit meetings or in peace conferences. It is not in Peking or Washington or the United Nations, but rather where a child of God prays in the power of the Spirit for God's will to be done in her life, in her home, and in the world around her.

Ruth Bell Graham

> *The effective prayer of a righteous man can accomplish much.*
> James 5:16 NASB

Two wings are necessary to lift our souls toward God: prayer and praise. Prayer asks. Praise accepts the answer.

Mrs. Charles E. Cowman

The Power of Perseverance

awesome verse!

Let us not become weary in doing good,
for at the proper time we will reap a harvest if we do not give up.

Galatians 6:9 NIV

Someone once said, "Life is a marathon, not a sprint." As you continue to search for purpose in everyday life (while, at the same time, balancing all your roles and responsibilities), you'll encounter your fair share of roadblocks and stumbling blocks. These situations require courage, patience, and above all, perseverance. As an example of perfect perseverance, you need look no further than your Savior, Jesus Christ.

Jesus, finished what He began. Despite the torture He endured, despite the shame of the cross, Jesus was steadfast in His faithfulness to God. We, too, must remain faithful, especially during times of hardship.

Are you tired? Ask God for strength. Are you discouraged? Believe in His promises. Are you frustrated or fearful? Pray as if everything depended upon God, and work as if everything depended upon you. With God's help, you will find the strength to be the kind of woman who makes your heavenly Father beam with pride.

Perhaps you are in a hurry for God to reveal His plans for your life. If so, be forewarned: God operates on His own timetable, not yours. Sometimes, God may answer your prayers with silence, and when He does, you must patiently persevere. In times of trouble, you must remain steadfast and trust in the merciful goodness of your Heavenly Father. Whatever your problem, He can handle it. Your job is to keep persevering until He does.

Your life is not a boring stretch of highway. It's a straight line to heaven. And just look at the fields ripening along the way. Look at the tenacity and endurance. Look at the grains of righteousness. You'll have quite a crop at harvest . . . so don't give up!

Joni Eareckson Tada

PRIORITIES FOR MY LIFE

If things don't work out at first, don't quit. If you never try, you'll never know how good you can be.

TIMELESS WISDOM FOR GODLY LIVING

We ought to make some progress, however little, every day, and show some increase of fervor. We ought to act as if we were at war—as, indeed, we are—and never relax until we have won the victory.

St. Teresa of Avila

God never gives up on you, so don't you ever give up on Him.

Marie T. Freeman

Little drops of water, little grains of sand; make the mighty ocean, and the pleasant land.

Julia Carnoy

Success actually becomes a habit through the determined overcoming of obstacles as we meet them one by one.

Laura Ingalls Wilder

For you have need of endurance, so that when you have done the will of God, you may receive what was promised.
Hebrews 10:36 NASB

Achieving that goal is a good feeling, but to get there you have to also get through the failures. You've got to be able to pick yourself up and continue.

Mary Lou Retton

MORE WORDS FROM GOD'S WORD

Thanks be to God! He gives us the victory through our Lord Jesus Christ. Therefore, my dear brothers, stand firm. Let nothing move you. Always give yourselves fully to the work of the Lord, because you know that your labor in the Lord is not in vain.

1 Corinthians 15:57-58 NIV

It is better to finish something than to start it. It is better to be patient than to be proud.

Ecclesiastes 7:8 NCV

Let us lay aside every weight and the sin that so easily ensnares us, and run with endurance the race that lies before us, keeping our eyes on Jesus, the source and perfecter of our faith.

Hebrews 12:1-2 Holman CSB

My Priorities for Life

I have a healthy respect for the power of perseverance.

When I am discouraged, I ask God to give me strength.

For me, it is helpful to associate with people who encourage me to be courageous, optimistic, energetic, and persistent.

Check Your Priority		
High	Med.	Low
—	—	—
—	—	—
—	—	—

Lonely in a Crowd

I am not alone, because the Father is with Me.

John 16:32 NKJV

If you're like most women, you've experienced occasional bouts of loneliness. If so, you understand the psychological pain that accompanies those feelings that "nobody cares." Of course, the real facts are seldom as desperate as you imagine them to be. In actuality, many people care about you, but at times, you may hardly notice their presence.

Sometimes, feelings of profound loneliness may be the result of untreated depression; in such cases medical intervention may be advisable. Other times, however, your feelings of loneliness may result from your own hesitation to "get out there and make new friends." Why might you hesitate to meet new people and make new friends? Perhaps you're naturally shy, and because of your shyness, you find it more difficult to interact with unfamiliar people. Or perhaps you're overly sensitive to the possibility of rejection. Oftentimes, this sensitivity to rejection results from low levels of self-esteem—you feel (quite incorrectly) that you are unworthy of the attentions of others. In truth, the world is literally teeming with people who are looking for new friends like you. Unfortunately, many of those people are insecure and lonely, so if you want to meet them, it's up to you to make the effort.

Writer Suzanne Dale Ezell observed, "Friends are like a quilt with lots of different shapes, sizes, colors, and patterns of fabric. But the end result brings you warmth and comfort in a support system that makes your life richer and fuller." And the American philosopher Ralph Waldo Emerson advised, "The only way to have a friend is to be one." Emerson realized that a lasting relationship, like a beautiful garden, must be tended with care. Here are a few helpful tips for tending the garden of friendship . . . and reaping a bountiful harvest:

Lasting friendships are governed by a rule . . . the Golden Rule. The best way to keep a friend is to treat that person like you want to be treated. (Matthew 7:12)

If you're trying to make new friends, become interested in them . . . and eventually they'll become interested in you. (Colossians 3:12)

Friendships take time. It takes time to make new friendships and time to cultivate old ones. But if you invest the time, you'll be glad you did . . . and so will they. (Philippians 1:3)

Get Involved: The more you involve yourself with various organizations (starting with your church), the better your chances to connect with lots of people. (1 Peter 5:2)

PRIORITIES FOR MY LIFE

Feeling lonely? If so, it's time to reach out . . . to other people and to God.

TIMELESS WISDOM FOR GODLY LIVING

When we are living apart for God, we can be lonely and lost, even in the midst of a crowd.

Billy Graham

We are born helpless. As soon as we are fully conscious we discover loneliness. We need others physically, emotionally, intellectually; we need them if we are to know anything, even ourselves.

C. S. Lewis

Most loneliness results from insulation rather than isolation.

James Dobson

Loneliness is the first thing which God's eye named as not good.

John Milton

The Lord is near all who call out to Him,
all who call out to Him with integrity.
He fulfills the desires of those who fear Him;
He hears their cry for help and saves them.
Psalm 145:18-19 Holman CSB

Are you feeling lonely today because of suffering? My word to you is simply this: Jesus Christ is there with you.

Warren Wiersbe

MORE WORDS FROM GOD'S WORD

Where can I go from your Spirit? Where can I flee from your presence? If I go up to the heavens, you are there; if I make my bed in the depths, you are there. If I rise on the wings of the dawn, if I settle on the far side of the sea, even there your hand will guide me, your right hand will hold me fast.

Psalm 139:7-10 NIV

I have set the Lord always before me; because He is at my right hand I shall not be moved.

Psalm 16:8 NKJV

No, I will not abandon you as orphans—I will come to you.

John 14:18 NLT

My Priorities for Life

	Check Your Priority	
High	Med.	Low

I believe that occasional periods of solitude can be beneficial to me.

— — —

I understand I can be lonely in a crowd—it is the quality of the relationships I have that count.

— — —

I know that the cure for loneliness may require that I be willing to reach out to others.

— — —

Accepting God's Abundance

And God will generously provide all you need.
Then you will always have everything you need
and plenty left over to share with others.

2 Corinthians 9:8 NLT

God's gifts are available to all, but they are not guaranteed; those gifts must be claimed by those who choose to follow Christ. As believers, we are free to accept God's gifts, or not; that choice, and the consequences that result from it, are ours and ours alone.

The 10th chapter of John tells us that Christ came to earth so that our lives might be filled with abundance. But what, exactly, did Jesus mean when He promised "life . . . more abundantly"? Was Jesus referring to material possessions or financial wealth? Hardly. When Jesus declared Himself the shepherd of mankind (John 10:7-9), He offered a different kind of abundance: a spiritual richness that extends beyond the temporal boundaries of this world.

If you are a thoughtful believer, you will open yourself to Christ's spiritual abundance by following Him completely and without reservation. When you do, you will receive the love, the peace, and the joy that He has promised.

The fullness of life in Christ is available to all who seek it and claim it. Count yourself among that number. Seek first the salvation that is available through a personal relationship with Jesus, and then claim the abundance that can—and should—be yours.

Do you sincerely seek the riches that our Savior offers to those who give themselves to Him? Then follow Him—and receive the blessings that He has promised. When you establish an intimate, passionate relationship with Christ, you are then free to claim the love, the protection, and the spiritual abundance that the Shepherd offers His sheep.

If we were given all we wanted here,
our hearts would settle for this world rather than the next.

Elisabeth Elliot

PRIORITIES FOR MY LIFE

Don't miss out on God's abundance: Every day is a beautifully wrapped gift from God. Unwrap it; use it; and give thanks to the Giver.

TIMELESS WISDOM FOR GODLY LIVING

Jesus intended for us to be overwhelmed by the blessings of
regular days. He said it was the reason he had come: "I am come
that they might have life, and that they might have it more
abundantly."

Gloria Gaither

God is the giver, and we are the receivers. And His richest gifts are
bestowed not upon those who do the greatest things, but upon
those who accept His abundance and His grace.

Hannah Whitall Smith

Get ready for God to show you not only His pleasure, but His
approval.

Joni Eareckson Tada

Come to terms with God and be at peace;
in this way good will come to you.
Job 22:21 Holman CSB

God has promised us abundance, peace, and eternal life. These
treasures are ours for the asking; all we must do is claim them.
One of the great mysteries of life is why on earth do so many of us
wait so very long to lay claim to God's gifts?

Marie T. Freeman

MORE WORDS FROM GOD'S WORD

Whoever has will be given more, and he will have an abundance.

Matthew 13:12 NIV

Ask and it will be given to you; seek and you will find; knock and the door will be opened to you. For everyone who asks receives; he who seeks finds; and to him who knocks, the door will be opened.

Matthew 7:7-8 NIV

The master was full of praise. "Well done, my good and faithful servant. You have been faithful in handling this small amount, so now I will give you many more responsibilities. Let's celebrate together!"

Matthew 25:21 NLT

My Priorities for Life

	Check Your Priority	
High	Med.	Low

I will trust that God's abundance is available to me.
— — —

I will obey God first and expect to receive His abundance second, not vice versa.
— — —

I will be a faithful steward of the resources that God chooses to place under my control.
— — —

I will work diligently to achieve my goals, and I will leave the rest up to God.
— — —

Trusting God's Word

Heaven and earth will pass away, but My words will never pass away.

Matthew 24:35 Holman CSB

God's promises are found in a book like no other: the Holy Bible. The Bible is a road map for life here on earth and for life eternal. As Christians, we are called upon to trust its promises, to follow its commandments, and to share its Good News.

As believers, we must study the Bible each day and meditate upon its meaning for our lives. Otherwise, we deprive ourselves of a priceless gift from our Creator. God's Holy Word is, indeed, a transforming, life-changing, one-of-a-kind treasure. And, a passing acquaintance with the Good Book is insufficient for Christians who seek to obey God's Word and to understand His will.

God has made promises to mankind and to you. God's promises never fail and they never grow old. You must trust those promises and share them with your family, with your friends, and with the world.

Are you standing on the promises of God? Are you expecting God to do wonderful things, or are you living beneath a cloud of apprehension and doubt? The familiar words of Psalm 118:24 remind us of a profound yet simple truth: "This is the day which the LORD hath made; we will rejoice and be glad in it" (KJV). Do you trust that promise, and do you live accordingly? If so, you are living the passionate life that God intends.

For passionate believers, every day begins and ends with God's Son and God's promises. When we accept Christ into our hearts, God promises us the opportunity for earthy peace and spiritual abundance. But more importantly, God promises us the priceless gift of eternal life.

As we face the inevitable challenges of life-here-on-earth, we must arm ourselves with the promises of God's Holy Word. When we do, we can expect the best, not only for the day ahead, but also for all eternity.

If we neglect the Bible, we cannot expect to benefit
from the wisdom and direction that result
from knowing God's Word.

Vonette Bright

PRIORITIES FOR MY LIFE

The Bible is the best-selling book of all time . . . for good reason. Ruth Bell Graham observed, "The Reference Point for the Christian is the Bible. All values, judgments, and attitudes must be gauged in relationship to this Reference Point." Make certain that you're an avid reader of God's best-seller, and make sure that you keep reading it as long as you live!

TIMELESS WISDOM FOR GODLY LIVING

God can see clearly no matter how dark or foggy the night is.
Trust His Word to guide you safely home.

Lisa Whelchel

God's Word is not merely letters on paper . . . it's alive. Believe
and draw near, for it longs to dance in your heart and whisper to
you in the night.

Lisa Bevere

I believe the reason so many are failing today is that they have not
disciplined themselves to read God's Word consistently, day in
and day out, and to apply it to every situation in life.

Kay Arthur

> *But the word of the Lord endures forever.*
> *And this is the word that was preached*
> *as the gospel to you.*
> 1 Peter 1:25 Holman CSB

For whatever life holds for you and your family in the coming
days, weave the unfailing fabric of God's Word through your heart
and mind. It will hold strong, even if the rest of life unravels.

Gigi Graham Tchividjian

MORE WORDS FROM GOD'S WORD

All Scripture is inspired by God and is profitable for teaching, for rebuking, for correcting, for training in righteousness, so that the man of God may be complete, equipped for every good work.

2 Timothy 3:16-17 Holman CSB

For the word of God is living and effective and sharper than any two-edged sword, penetrating as far as to divide soul, spirit, joints, and marrow; it is a judge of the ideas and thoughts of the heart.

Hebrews 4:12 Holman CSB

So then faith comes by hearing, and hearing by the word of God.

Romans 10:17 NKJV

My Priorities for Life

I understand that wisdom is found in God's Word, and I seek to gain God's wisdom through daily Bible readings.

I believe that "head knowledge" is important, but that "heart knowledge" is imperative.

I believe that God's Word should be the instruction book for all of mankind and for me.

Check Your Priority		
High	Med.	Low
—	—	—
—	—	—
—	—	—

God's Perfect Love

We know how much God loves us,
and we have put our trust in him. God is love,
and all who live in love live in God, and God lives in them.

1 John 4:16 NLT

God's love for you is bigger and better than you can imagine. In fact, God's love is far too big to comprehend (in this lifetime). But this much we know: God loves you so much that He sent His Son Jesus to come to this earth and to die for you. And, when you accepted Jesus into your heart, God gave you a gift that is more precious than gold: the gift of eternal life.

The words of Romans 8 make this promise: "For I am persuaded that neither death nor life, nor angels nor principalities nor powers, nor things present nor things to come, nor height nor depth, nor any other created thing, shall be able to separate us from the love of God which is in Christ Jesus our Lord" (38-39 NKJV).

Sometimes, in the crush of your daily duties, God may seem far away, but He is not. God is everywhere you have ever been and everywhere you will ever go. He is with you night and day; He knows your thoughts and He hears your prayers. When you earnestly seek Him, you will find Him because He is here, waiting patiently for you to reach out to Him.

Reach out to God today and always. Encourage your family members to do likewise. And then, arm-in-arm with your loved ones, praise God for blessings that are simply too numerous to count.

Everything I possess of any worth is
a direct product of God's love.

Beth Moore

Being loved by Him whose opinion matters most gives us
the security to risk loving, too—even loving ourselves.

Gloria Gaither

PRIORITIES FOR MY LIFE

When you invite the love of God into your heart, everything changes . . . including you.

TIMELESS WISDOM FOR GODLY LIVING

The unfolding of our friendship with the Father will be a never-ending revelation stretching on into eternity.

Catherine Marshall

There is no pit so deep that God's love is not deeper still.

Corrie ten Boom

The fact is, God no longer deals with us in judgment but in mercy. If people got what they deserved, this old planet would have ripped apart at the seams centuries ago. Praise God that because of His great love "we are not consumed, for his compassions never fail (Lam. 3:22).

Joni Eareckson Tada

> *As the Father loved Me,*
> *I also have loved you; abide in My love.*
> John 15:9 NKJV

Accepting God's love as a gift instead of trying to earn it had somehow seemed presumptuous and arrogant to me, when, in fact, my pride was tricking me into thinking that I could merit His love and forgiveness with my own strength.

Lisa Whelchel

MORE WORDS FROM GOD'S WORD

For God so loved the world, that he gave his only begotten Son, that whosoever believeth in him should not perish, but have everlasting life.

John 3:16 KJV

The unfailing love of the LORD never ends! By his mercies we have been kept from complete destruction.

Lamentations 3:22 NLT

His banner over me was love.

Song of Solomon 2:4 KJV

For he chose us in him before the creation of the world to be holy and blameless in his sight. In love he predestined us to be adopted as his sons through Jesus Christ, in accordance with his pleasure and will....

Ephesians 1:4-5 NIV

My Priorities for Life

	Check Your Priority	
High	Med.	Low

I believe God loves me.

— — —

I believe God wants me to love Him in return.

— — —

I believe that the more I worship God, the more that I study His Word, and the more time that I spend quietly with Him, the more I will sense His presence and His love.

— — —

Putting Faith to the Test

For whatever is born of God overcomes the world.
And this is the victory that has overcome the world—our faith.

1 John 5:4 NKJV

When a suffering woman sought healing by merely touching the hem of His cloak, Jesus replied, "Daughter, be of good comfort; thy faith hath made thee whole" (Matthew 9:22 KJV). Christ's message is clear: we should live by faith. But, when we face adversity, illness, or heartbreak, living by faith can be difficult indeed. Yet this much is certain: whatever our circumstances, we must continue to plant the seeds of faith in our hearts, trusting that in time God will bring forth a bountiful harvest.

Have you, on occasion, felt your faith in God slipping away? If so, consider yourself a member of a very large club. We, human beings are subject to an assortment of negative emotions such as fear, worry, anxiety, and doubt. When we fall short of perfect faith, God understands us and forgives us. And, God stands ready to strengthen us if we turn our doubts and fears over to Him.

As you enter into the next phase of your life, you'll face many experiences: some good, and some not so good. When the sun is shining and all is well, it is easier to have faith. But, when life takes an unexpected turn for the worse, as it will from time to time, your faith will be tested. In times of trouble and doubt, God remains faithful to you. Do the same for Him.

Are you tapped in to the power of faith? Hopefully so. The hours that you invest in Bible study, prayer, meditation, and worship should be times of enrichment and celebration. And, if your faith is being tested to the point of breaking, know that your Savior is near. Reach out to Him, and let Him heal your broken spirit. Be content to touch even the smallest fragment of the Master's garment, and He will make you whole.

Faith is seeing light with the eyes of your heart,
when the eyes of your body see only darkness.

Barbara Johnson

PRIORITIES FOR MY LIFE

Faith is more than a feeling. Faith sometimes results in good feelings, but as Kay Arthur correctly observes, "We are to live by faith, not feelings."

TIMELESS WISDOM FOR GODLY LIVING

Joy is faith feasting and celebrating the One in Whom it trusts.

Susan Lenzkes

I want my life to be a faith-filled leap into his arms, knowing he will be there—not that everything will go as I want, but that he will be there and that this will be enough.

Sheila Walsh

If God chooses to remain silent, faith is content.

Ruth Bell Graham

Faith is putting all your eggs in God's basket, then counting your blessings before they hatch.

Ramona C. Carroll

It is impossible to please God apart from faith. And why? Because anyone who wants to approach God must believe both that he exists and that he cares enough to respond to those who seek him.

Hebrews 11:6 MSG

Faith is the quiet place within us where we don't get whiplash every time life tosses us a curve.

Patsy Clairmont

MORE WORDS FROM GOD'S WORD

Anything is possible if a person believes.

Mark 9:23 NLT

Fight the good fight of faith; take hold of the eternal life to which you were called....

1 Timothy 6:12 NASB

Have faith in the LORD your God and you will be upheld....

2 Chronicles 20:20 NIV

Therefore, being always of good courage . . . we walk by faith, not by sight.

2 Corinthians 5:6-7 NASB

I have fought the good fight, I have finished the race, I have kept the faith.

2 Timothy 4:7 NIV

My Priorities for Life

| | Check Your Priority | |
High	Med.	Low

I believe in the power of faith to "make me whole."

— — —

My faith is stronger when I keep my eyes on Jesus and not on my circumstances.

— — —

I believe that faith is a choice, and I choose to have faith.

— — —

Energy for Today

Never be lacking in zeal,
but keep your spiritual fervor, serving the Lord.

Romans 12:11 NIV

All of us have moments when we feel drained. All of us suffer through difficult days, trying times, and perplexing periods of our lives. Thankfully, God stands ready and willing to give us comfort and strength if we turn to Him.

Burning the candle at both ends is tempting but potentially destructive. Instead, we should place first things first by saying no to the things that we simply don't have the time or the energy to do. As we establish our priorities, we should turn to God and to His Holy Word for guidance.

Are you an energized Christian? You should be. But if you're not, you must seek strength and renewal from the one source that will never fail: that source, of course, is your Heavenly Father. And rest assured—when you sincerely petition Him, He will give you all the strength you need to live victoriously for Him.

If you're a woman with too many demands and too few hours in which to meet them, don't fret. Instead, focus upon God and upon His love for you. Then, ask Him for the wisdom to prioritize your life and the strength to fulfill your responsibilities. God will give you the energy to do the most important things on today's to-do list . . . if you ask Him. So ask Him.

When the dream of our heart is one that God has
planted there, a strange happiness flows into us.
At that moment, all of the spiritual resources of
the universe are released to help us. Our praying is then
at one with the will of God and becomes a channel for
the Creator's purposes for us and our world.

Catherine Marshall

PRIORITIES FOR MY LIFE

Feeling exhausted? Try this: Start getting more sleep each night; begin a program of regular, sensible exercise; avoid harmful food and drink; and turn your problems over to God . . . and the greatest of these is "turn your problems over to God."

TIMELESS WISDOM FOR GODLY LIVING

Worry does not empty tomorrow of its sorrow; it empties today of its strength.

Corrie ten Boom

Our Lord never drew power from Himself, He drew it always from His Father.

Oswald Chambers

Love the moment and the energy of the moment will spread beyond all boundaries.

Corita Kent

The world belongs to the energetic.

Ralph Waldo Emerson

Whatever work you do, do your best, because you are going to the grave, where there is no working . . . .
Ecclesiastes 9:10 NCV

It is God's love for us that causes Him to bring us to the end of our own strength. He sees our need to trust Him.

Charles Swindoll

MORE WORDS FROM GOD'S WORD

Those who hope in the LORD will renew their strength. They will soar on wings like eagles; they will run and not grow weary, they will walk and not be faint.

Isaiah 40:31 NIV

He did it with all his heart. So he prospered.

2 Chronicles 31:21 NKJV

Now we want each of you to demonstrate the same diligence for the final realization of your hope, so that you won't become lazy, but imitators of those who inherit the promises through faith and perseverance.

Hebrews 6:11-12 Holman CSB

My Priorities for Life

I place my hope and trust in God, and when I am weary or discouraged, I will turn to Him.

I eat sensibly and exercise regularly.

I manage my daily activities in a way that allows me to get adequate sleep each night.

I do the work that needs to be done today, and I try not to focus my thoughts and energies on the regrets of yesterday or the uncertainties of tomorrow.

Check Your Priority		
High	Med.	Low
—	—	—
—	—	—
—	—	—
—	—	—

When People Are Difficult

Real wisdom, God's wisdom, begins with a holy life
and is characterized by getting along with others.
It is gentle and reasonable, overflowing with mercy and blessings,
not hot one day and cold the next, not two-faced.

James 3:17 MSG

All of us can be grumpy, hardheaded, and difficult to deal with at times. When you have occasion to deal with difficult people (and you will), the following tips should help:

1. Do Make Sure That You're Not the One Being Difficult: Perhaps the problems that concern you have their origin, at least partially, within your own heart. If so, fix yourself first. (Philippians 2:3)

2. Don't Try to Change the Other Person: Unless the person you're trying to change is a young child, and unless you are that child's parent or guardian, don't try to change him or her. Why? Because teenagers and adults change when they want to, not when you want them to. (Proverbs 10:14)

3. Do Insist Upon Logical Consequences to Irresponsible Behavior: When you protect other people from the

consequences of their misbehavior, you're doing those folks a profound disservice. Most people don't learn new behaviors until the old behaviors stop working, so don't be an enabler. (Hebrews 12:5-6)

4. Don't Allow Yourself to Become Caught Up in the Other Person's Emotional Outbursts: If someone is ranting, raving, or worse, you have the right to excuse yourself and leave. Remember: emotions are highly contagious, so if the other person is angry, you will soon become angry, too. Instead of adding your own emotional energy to the outburst, you should make the conscious effort to remain calm—and part of remaining calm may be leaving the scene. (Proverbs 22:24-25)

And finally, when you've finished dealing with that difficult person, do your best to forget about the confrontation. Everybody's human, and everybody needs forgiveness.

You can be sure you are abiding in Christ if you are able to have a Christlike love toward the people that irritate you the most.

Vonette Bright

PRIORITIES FOR MY LIFE

Don't allow yourself to become a difficult person to be around: You'll never whine, complain, moan, or groan your way to happiness, so don't even try.

TIMELESS WISDOM FOR GODLY LIVING

When something robs you of your peace of mind, ask yourself if it is worth the energy you are expending on it. If not, then put it out of your mind in an act of discipline. Every time the thought of "it" returns, refuse it.

Kay Arthur

One way or the other, God, who thought up the family in the first place, has the very best idea of how to bring sense to the chaos of broken relationships we see all around us. I really believe that if I remain still and listen a lot, He will share some solutions with me so I can share them with others.

Jill Briscoe

Sour godliness is the devil's religion.

John Wesley

You have heard it said, "Love your neighbor and hate your enemy." But I tell you: Love your enemies and pray for those who persecute you, that you may be sons of your Father in heaven.
Matthew 5:43-45 NIV

We are all fallen creatures and all very hard to live with.

C. S. Lewis

MORE WORDS FROM GOD'S WORD

Hatred stirs up trouble, but love forgives all wrongs.

Proverbs 10:12 NCV

Escape quickly from the company of fools; they're a waste of your time, a waste of your words.

Proverbs 14:7 MSG

Smart people are patient; they will be honored if they ignore insults.

Proverbs 19:11 NCV

Do not gloat when your enemy falls; when he stumbles, do not let your heart rejoice.

Proverbs 24:17 NIV

My Priorities for Life

I will work hard at forgiving difficult people; when I am successful, I find peace.

I refuse to allow myself to become caught up in other people's emotional outbursts.

Whenever possible, I try to look at the humorous side of life, including some of the absurd behaviors that I witness from time to time.

Check Your Priority		
High	Med.	Low
—	—	—
—	—	—
—	—	—

The Wisdom To Be Hopeful

The lines of purpose in your lives never grow slack,
tightly tied as they are to your future in heaven, kept taut by hope.

Colossians 1:5 MSG

On the darkest days of our lives, we may be confronted with an illusion that seems very real indeed: the illusion of hopelessness. Try though we might, we simply can't envision a solution to our problems—and we fall into the darkness of despair. During these times, we may question God—His love, His presence, even His very existence. Despite God's promises, despite Christ's love, and despite our many blessings, we may envision little or no hope for the future. These dark days can be dangerous times for us and for our loved ones.

If you find yourself falling into the spiritual traps of worry and discouragement, seek the encouraging words of fellow Christians, and the healing touch of Jesus. After all, it was Christ who promised, "These things I have spoken unto you, that in me ye might have peace. In the world ye shall have tribulation: but be of good cheer; I have overcome the world" (John 16:33 KJV).

Can you place your future into the hands of a loving and all-knowing God? Can you live amid the uncertainties of today, knowing that God has dominion over all your tomorrows? Can you summon the faith to trust God in good times and hard times? If you can, you are wise and you are blessed.

Once you've made the decision to trust God completely, it's time to get busy. The willingness to take action—even if the outcome of that action is uncertain—is an effective way to combat hopelessness. When you decide to roll up your sleeves and begin solving your own problems, you'll feel empowered, and you may see the first real glimmer of hope.

If you're waiting for someone else to solve your problems, or if you're waiting for God to patch things up by Himself, you may become impatient, despondent, or both. But when you stop waiting and start working, God has a way of pitching in and finishing the job. The advice of American publisher Cyrus Curtis still rings true: "Believe in the Lord and He will do half the work—the last half."

So, today and every day, ask God for these things: clear perspective, mountain-moving faith, and the courage to do what needs doing. After all, no problem is too big for God—not even yours.

PRIORITIES FOR MY LIFE

Remember: other people have experienced the same kind of hard times you may be experiencing now. They made it, and so can you.

TIMELESS WISDOM FOR GODLY LIVING

And still today, when you boil it all down, our message to the world—even to the world that comes disguised as our child's schoolteacher, our next-door neighbor, or our personal hair stylist—is hope. Hope beyond the slavery of sin. And hope beyond the grave.

Becky Tirabassi

God's Word never said we were not to grieve our losses. It says we are not to grieve as those who have no hope (1 Thessalonians 4:13). Big Difference.

Beth Moore

God is the only one who can make the valley of trouble a door of hope.

Catherine Marshall

Let us hold fast the confession of our hope without wavering, for He who promised is faithful.
Hebrews 10:23 NASB

Hope is the desire and the ability to move forward.

Emilie Barnes

MORE WORDS FROM GOD'S WORD

Now faith is the substance of things hoped for, the evidence of things not seen.

Hebrews 11:1 KJV

This hope we have as an anchor of the soul, a hope both sure and steadfast.

Hebrews 6:19 NASB

Full of hope, you'll relax, confident again; you'll look around, sit back, and take it easy.

Job 11:18 MSG

May the God of hope fill you with all joy and peace as you trust in him, so that you may overflow with hope by the power of the Holy Spirit.

Romans 15:13 NIV

My Priorities for Life

I believe that genuine hope begins with hope in a sovereign God.

I have found that action is an antidote to worry.

I believe that God offers me "a peace that passes understanding," and I desire to accept God's peace.

Check Your Priority		
High	Med.	Low
—	—	—
—	—	—
—	—	—

Discovering God's Peace

I leave you peace; my peace I give you.
I do not give it to you as the world does.
So don't let your hearts be troubled or afraid.

John 14:27 NCV

Have you found the lasting peace that can—and should—be yours through Jesus Christ? Or are you still chasing the illusion of "peace and happiness" that the world promises but cannot deliver?

The beautiful words of John 14:27 promise that Jesus offers peace, not as the world gives, but as He alone gives. Your challenge is to accept Christ's peace and then, as best you can, to share His peace with your neighbors. But sometimes, that's easier said than done.

If you are a person with lots of obligations and plenty of responsibilities, it is simply a fact of life: You worry. From time to time, you worry about finances, safety, health, home, family, or about countless other concerns, some great and some small. Where is the best place to take your worries? Take them to God . . . and leave them there.

The Scottish preacher George McDonald observed, "It has been well said that no man ever sank under the burden of the day. It is when tomorrow's burden is added to the burden of today that the weight is more than a man can bear. Never load yourselves so, my friends. If you find yourselves so loaded, at least remember this: it is your own doing, not God's. He begs you to leave the future to Him."

Today, as a gift to yourself, to your family, and to your friends, claim the inner peace that is your spiritual birthright: the peace of Jesus Christ. Christ is standing at the door, waiting patiently for you to invite Him to reign over your heart. His eternal peace is offered freely. Claim it today.

When we do what is right, we have contentment, peace, and happiness.

Beverly LaHaye

PRIORITIES FOR MY LIFE

Sometimes peace is a scarce commodity in a demanding, 21st century world. How can we find the peace that we so desperately desire? By turning our days and our lives over to God. Elisabeth Elliot writes, "If my life is surrendered to God, all is well. Let me not grab it back, as though it were in peril in His hand but would be safer in mine!" May we give our lives, our hopes, and our prayers to the Father, and, by doing so, accept His will and His peace.

TIMELESS WISDOM FOR GODLY LIVING

Look around you and you'll be distressed; look within yourself and you'll be depressed; look at Jesus, and you'll be at rest!

Corrie ten Boom

There may be no trumpet sound or loud applause when we make a right decision, just a calm sense of resolution and peace.

Gloria Gaither

We need to be at peace with our past, content with our present, and sure about our future, knowing they are all in God's hands.

Joyce Meyer

Peace and love are always alive in us, but we are not always alive to peace and love.

Juliana of Norwich

If your sinful nature controls your mind, there is death. But if the Holy Spirit controls your mind, there is life and peace.

Romans 8:6 NLT

God has revealed to us a new reality that the world does not understand: In His eternal kingdom, what matters is being like our Father. That is the way to success and peace.

Mary Morrison Suggs

MORE WORDS FROM GOD'S WORD

If it is possible, as far as it depends on you, live at peace with everyone.

Romans 12:18 NIV

And the peace of God, which surpasses all understanding, will guard your hearts and minds through Christ Jesus. Finally, brethren, whatever things are true, whatever things are noble, whatever things are just, whatever things are pure, whatever things are lovely, whatever things are of good report, if there is any virtue and if there is anything praiseworthy— meditate on these things.

Philippians 4:7-8 NKJV

Blessed are the peacemakers, for they will be called sons of God.

Matthew 5:9 NIV

My Priorities for Life

	Check Your Priority	
High	Med.	Low

I understand the value of living a peaceful life.

— — —

Experience teaches me that peace is found by living in the center of God's will.

— — —

I find that the more time I spend in prayer, the more peaceful I feel.

— — —

A Faith Bigger Than Fear

Jesus said, "Don't let your hearts be troubled.
Trust in God, and trust in me."

John 14:1 NCV

If you are like most women, it's simply a fact of life: from time to time, you worry. You worry about health, about finances, about safety, about relationships, about family, and about countless other challenges of life, some great and some small.

Because of His humanity, Jesus understood the inevitability of worry. And He addressed the topic clearly and forcefully in the 6th chapter of Matthew:

Therefore I say to you, do not worry about your life, what you will eat or what you will drink; nor about your body, what you will put on. Is not life more than food and the body more than clothing? Look at the birds of the air, for they neither sow nor reap nor gather into barns; yet your heavenly Father feeds them. Are you not of more value than they? Which of you by worrying can add one cubit to his stature? . . . Therefore do not worry about tomorrow, for tomorrow will worry about its own things. Sufficient for the day is its own trouble. V. 25-27, 34 NKJV

More often than not, our worries stem from an inability to focus and to trust. We fail to focus on a priceless gift from God:

the profound, precious, present moment. Instead of thanking God for the blessings of this day, we choose to fret about two more ominous days: yesterday and tomorrow. We stew about the unfairness of the past, or we agonize about the uncertainty of the future. Such thinking stirs up negative feelings that prepare our hearts and minds for an equally destructive emotion: fear.

Our fears are also rooted in a failure to trust. Instead of trusting God's plans for our lives, we fix our minds on countless troubles that might come to pass (but seldom do). A better strategy, of course, is to take God at His Word by trusting His promises. Our Lord has promised that He will care for our needs—needs, by the way, that He understands far more completely than we do. God's Word is unambiguous; so, too, should be our trust in Him.

In Matthew 6, Jesus reminds us that each day has enough worries of its own without the added weight of yesterday's regrets or tomorrow's fears. That's a message worth remembering. So the next time you're tempted to worry about the mistakes of yesterday or the uncertainties of tomorrow, turn your heart toward God. Take your troubles to Him; take your fears to Him; take your doubts to Him; take your weaknesses to Him; take your sorrows to Him . . . and leave them all there. Seek protection from the One who offers you eternal salvation; build your spiritual house upon the Rock that cannot be moved.

PRIORITIES FOR MY LIFE

Carefully divide your areas of concern into two categories: those you can control and those you cannot. Resolve never to waste time or energy worrying about the latter.

TIMELESS WISDOM FOR GODLY LIVING

Worship and worry cannot live in the same heart; they are mutually exclusive.

Ruth Bell Graham

Submit each day to God, knowing that He is God over all your tomorrows.

Kay Arthur

God is great; God is good; God loves you, and He sent His Son to die for your sins. When you keep these things in mind, you'll discover that it's hard to stay worried for long.

Marie T. Freeman

Come to Me, all you who labor and are heavy laden, and I will give you rest. Take My yoke upon you and learn from Me, for I am gentle and lowly in heart, and you will find rest for your souls. For My yoke is easy and My burden is light.
Matthew 11:28-30 NKJV

He treats us as sons, and all He asks in return is that we shall treat Him as a Father whom we can trust without anxiety. We must take the son's place of dependence and trust, and we must let Him keep the father's place of care and responsibility.

Hannah Whitall Smith

MORE WORDS FROM GOD'S WORD

I was very worried, but you comforted me . . . .

Psalm 94:19 NCV

An anxious heart weighs a man down....

Proverbs 12:25 NIV

Don't fret or worry. Instead of worrying, pray. Let petitions and praises shape your worries into prayers, letting God know your concerns. Before you know it, a sense of God's wholeness, everything coming together for good, will come and settle you down. It's wonderful what happens when Christ displaces worry at the center of your life.

Philippians 4:6-7 MSG

My Priorities for Life

I believe that it is important to try to live in "day-tight" compartments by not fretting too much about yesterday or tomorrow.

I use prayer as an antidote to worry.

When I am worried, I try to think of things that I can to help solve the things that trouble me.

Check Your Priority		
High	Med.	Low
—	—	—
—	—	—
—	—	—

The Wisdom to Give Thanks

In everything give thanks;
for this is the will of God in Christ Jesus for you.

1 Thessalonians 5:18 NKJV

God has blessed us beyond measure, and we owe Him everything, including our constant praise. That's why thanksgiving should become a habit, a regular part of our daily routines. When we slow down and express our gratitude to the One who made us, we enrich our own lives and the lives of those around us.

Dietrich Bonhoeffer observed, "It is only with gratitude that life becomes rich." These words most certainly apply to you.

As a follower of Christ, you have been blessed beyond measure. God sent His only Son to die for you. And, God has given you the priceless gifts of eternal love and eternal life. You, in turn, should approach your Heavenly Father with reverence and gratitude.

Are you a thankful person? Do you appreciate the gifts that God has given you? And, do you demonstrate your gratitude by being a faithful steward of the gifts and talents that you have received from your Creator? You most certainly should be thankful. After all, when you stop to think about it, God has given you more blessings than you can count. So the question of the day is this: will you thank your Heavenly Father . . . or will you spend your time and energy doing other things?

God is always listening—are you willing to say thanks? It's up to you, and the next move is yours.

Go outside, to the fields, enjoy nature and the sunshine,
go out and try to recapture happiness in yourself and in God.
Think of all the beauty that's still left
in and around you and be happy!

Anne Frank

PRIORITIES FOR MY LIFE

Make your feelings known to God. Of course you are thankful to God for all His blessings, starting, of course, with your family and your friends. Tell Him so.

TIMELESS WISDOM FOR GODLY LIVING

We give strength to our souls as we train ourselves to speak words of thankfulness and praise.

Annie Chapman

Every day has its own particular brand of holiness to discover and worship appropriately.

Annie Dillard

The game was to just find something about everything to be glad about—no matter what it was. You see, when you're hunting for the glad things, you sort of forget the other kind.

Eleanor H. Porter

Our prayers for you are always spilling over into thanksgivings. We can't quit thanking God our Father and Jesus our Messiah for you!
Colossians 1:3 MSG

One reason why we don't thank God for his answer to our prayer is that frequently we don't recognize them as being answers to our prayers. We just take his bountiful supply or dramatic action for granted when it comes.

Evelyn Christenson

MORE WORDS FROM GOD'S WORD

My counsel for you is simple and straightforward: Just go ahead with what you've been given. You received Christ Jesus, the Master; now live him. You're deeply rooted in him. You're well constructed upon him. You know your way around the faith. Now do what you've been taught. School's out; quit studying the subject and start living it! And let your living spill over into thanksgiving.

Colossians 2:6-7 MSG

Finally, brethren, whatsoever things are true, whatsoever things are honest, whatsoever things are just, whatsoever things are pure, whatsoever things are lovely, whatsoever things are of good report; if there be any virtue, and if there be any praise, think on these things.

Philippians 4:8 KJV

Thanks be to God for His indescribable gift!

2 Corinthians 9:15 NKJV

My Priorities for Life

I believe that giving thanks to God helps me keep things in proper perspective.

I believe that it is important to show others what it means to be a thankful Christian.

I take time each day to count my many blessings.

Check Your Priority		
High	Med.	Low
—	—	—
—	—	—
—	—	—

Power of Optimism

But if we look forward to something we don't have yet,
we must wait patiently and confidently.

Romans 8:25 NLT

Are you a hope-filled, enthusiastic Christian? You should be. After all, as a believer, you have every reason to be optimistic about your life here on earth and your eternal life in heaven. As English clergyman William Ralph Inge observed, "No Christian should be a pessimist, for Christianity is a system of radical optimism." Inge's words are most certainly true, but sometimes, you may find yourself pulled down by the inevitable concerns of everyday life. If you find yourself discouraged, exhausted, or both, then it's time to ask yourself this question: what's bothering you, and why?

If you're overly worried by the inevitable ups and downs of life, God wants to have a little chat with you. After all, God has made promises to you that He intends to keep. And if your life has been transformed by God's only begotten Son, then you, as a recipient of God's grace, have every reason to live courageously.

Are you willing to trust God's plans for your life? Hopefully, you will trust Him completely. After all, the words of the Psalmist make it clear: "The ways of God are without fault. The Lord's words are pure. He is a shield to those who trust him" (Psalm 18:30 NCV). These words should serve as a reminder that even when the challenges of the day seem daunting, God remains steadfast. And, so should you.

So make this promise to yourself and keep it—vow to be an expectant, faith-filled Christian. Think optimistically about your life, your profession, your family, your future, and your purpose for living. Trust your hopes, not your fears. Take time to celebrate God's glorious creation. And then, when you've filled your heart with hope and gladness, share your optimism with others. They'll be better for it, and so will you.

If you can't tell whether your glass is half-empty or half-full, you don't need another glass; what you need is better eyesight . . . and a more thankful heart.

Marie T. Freeman

PRIORITIES FOR MY LIFE

Be a realistic optimist: You should strive to think realistically about the future, but you should never confuse realism with pessimism. Your attitude toward the future will help create your future, so you might as well put the self-fulfilling prophecy to work for you by being both a realist and an optimist. And remember that life is far too short to be a pessimist.

TIMELESS WISDOM FOR GODLY LIVING

Dark as my path may seem to others, I carry a magic light in my heart. Faith, the spiritual strong searchlight, illumines the way, and although sinister doubts lurk in the shadow, I walk unafraid toward the enchanted wood where the foliage is always green, where joy abides, where nightingales nest and sing, and where life and death are one in the presence of the Lord.

Helen Keller

We may run, walk, stumble, drive, or fly, but let us never lose sight of the reason for the journey, or miss a chance to see a rainbow on the way.

Gloria Gaither

Make the least of all that goes and the most of all that comes. Don't regret what is past. Cherish what you have. Look forward to all that is to come. And most important of all, rely moment by moment on Jesus Christ.

Gigi Graham Tchividjian

Make me hear joy and gladness.
Psalm 51:8 NKJV

The Christian lifestyle is not one of legalistic do's and don'ts, but one that is positive, attractive, and joyful.

Vonette Bright

MORE WORDS FROM GOD'S WORD

My cup runs over. Surely goodness and mercy shall follow me all the days of my life; and I will dwell in the house of the Lord forever.

Psalm 23:5-6 NKJV

For God has not given us a spirit of fear, but of power and of love and of a sound mind.

2 Timothy 1:7 NLT

The Lord is my light and my salvation; whom shall I fear? The Lord is the strength of my life; of whom shall I be afraid?

Psalm 27:1 KJV

My Priorities for Life

	Check Your Priority		
	High	Med.	Low
I understand the importance of counting my blessings, not my hardships.	—	—	—
I will look for opportunities, not obstructions; and I will look for possibilities, not problems.	—	—	—
I understand the need to associate with people who encourage me to be optimistic, upbeat, and cheerful.	—	—	—
I will share words of encouragement and hope with my family, with my friends, and with my coworkers.	—	—	—

Making All Things New

*The One who was sitting on the throne said,
"Look! I am making everything new!" Then he said,
"Write this, because these words are true and can be trusted."*

Revelation 21:5 NCV

For busy women living in a fast-paced 21st century world, life may seem like a merry-go-round that never stops turning. If that description seems to fit your life, then you may find yourself running short of patience, or strength, or both. If you're feeling tired or discouraged, there is a source from which you can draw the power needed to recharge your spiritual batteries. That source is God.

Are you exhausted or troubled? Turn your heart toward God in prayer. Are you weak or worried? Take the time—or, more accurately, make the time—to delve deeply into God's Holy Word. Are you spiritually depleted? Call upon fellow believers to support you, and call upon Christ to renew your spirit and your life. When you do, you'll discover that the Creator of the universe stands always ready and always able to create a new sense of wonderment and joy in you.

But while relaxation is one thing, refreshment is another.
We need to drink frequently and at length from
God's fresh springs, to spend time in the Scripture,
time in fellowship with Him, time worshiping Him.

Ruth Bell Graham

But those who wait on the Lord Shall renew their strength;
They shall mount up with wings like eagles,
They shall run and not be weary,
They shall walk and not faint.

Isaiah 40:31 NKJV

PRIORITIES FOR MY LIFE

Do you need time for yourself? Take it. Ruth Bell Graham
observed, "It is important that we take time out for ourselves—for
relaxation, for refreshment." Enough said.

TIMELESS WISDOM FOR GODLY LIVING

He is the God of wholeness and restoration.

Stormie Omartian

Repentance removes old sins and wrong attitudes, and it opens the way for the Holy Spirit to restore our spiritual health.

Shirley Dobson

When we reach the end of our strength, wisdom, and personal resources, we enter into the beginning of his glorious provisions.

Patsy Clairmont

> *When doubts filled my mind,*
> *your comfort gave me renewed hope and cheer.*
> Psalm 94:19 NLT

Each of us has something broken in our lives: a broken promise, a broken dream, a broken marriage, a broken heart . . . and we must decide how we're going to deal with our brokenness. We can wallow in self-pity or regret, accomplishing nothing and having no fun or joy in our circumstances; or we can determine with our will to take a few risks, get out of our comfort zone, and see what God will do to bring unexpected delight in our time of need.

Luci Swindoll

MORE WORDS FROM GOD'S WORD

Create in me a pure heart, O God, and renew a steadfast spirit within me. Do not cast me from your presence or take your Holy Spirit from me. Restore to me the joy of your salvation and grant me a willing spirit, to sustain me.

Psalm 51:10-12 NIV

He makes me to lie down in green pastures; He leads me beside the still waters. He restores my soul; He leads me in the paths of righteousness For His name's sake.

Psalm 23:2–3 NKJV

Therefore if anyone is in Christ, he is a new creature; the old things passed away; behold, new things have come.

2 Corinthians 5:17 Holman CSB

My Priorities for Life

I believe that God can make all things new . . . including me.

I take time each day to be still and let God give me perspective and direction.

I understand the importance of getting sensible exercise and a sensible amount of sleep each night.

Check Your Priority		
High	Med.	Low
—	—	—
—	—	—
—	—	—

A Principled Life

Sow righteousness for yourselves and reap faithful love;
break up your untilled ground. It is time to seek the Lord
until He comes and sends righteousness on you like the rain.

Hosea 10:12 Holman CSB

Whether you realize it or not, your life is shaped by your values. From the time your alarm clock wakes you in the morning until the moment you lay your head on the pillow at night, your actions are guided by the values that you hold most dear. If you're a thoughtful believer, then those values are shaped by the Word of God.

Society seeks to impose its set of values upon you, however these values are often contrary to God's Word (and thus contrary to your own best interests). The world makes promises that it simply cannot fulfill. It promises happiness, contentment, prosperity, and abundance. But genuine abundance is not a by-product of possessions or status; it is a by-product of your thoughts, your actions, and your relationship with God. The world's promises are incomplete and deceptive; God's promises are unfailing. Your challenge, then, is to build your value system upon the firm foundation of God's promises . . . nothing else will suffice.

Each day, you make countless decisions, decisions that hopefully can bring you into a closer relationship with your

Heavenly Father. When God's values become your values, then you share in His abundance and His peace. But, if you place the world's priorities in front of God's priorities, you're asking for trouble . . . BIG trouble.

As a citizen of the 21st Century, you live in a world that is filled with countless opportunities to make big-time mistakes. The world seems to cry, "Worship me with your time, your money, your energy, and your thoughts!" But God commands otherwise: He commands you to worship Him and Him alone; everything else must be secondary.

Do you want to experience God's peace and His blessings? If so, then you must build your life upon a value system that puts God first. So, when you're faced with a difficult choice or a powerful temptation, seek God's counsel and trust the counsel that He gives. Invite God into your heart and live according to His commandments. Study His Word and talk to Him often. When you do, you will share in the abundance and peace that only God can give.

PRIORITIES FOR MY LIFE

Since your personal value system will determine the quality and direction of your life, you must choose those values carefully; and you should choose them in accordance with God's commandments.

TIMELESS WISDOM FOR GODLY LIVING

People can't live with change if there's not a changeless core inside them. The key to the ability to change is a changeless sense of who you are, what you are about and what you value.

Stephen Covey

Sadly, family problems and even financial problems are seldom the real problem, but often the symptom of a weak or nonexistent value system.

Dave Ramsey

If you want to be proactive in the way you live your life, if you want to influence your life's direction, if you want your life to exhibit the qualities you find desirable, and if you want to live with integrity, then you need to know what your values are, decide to embrace them, and practice them every day.

John Maxwell

> *Teach me, O Lord, the way of Your statutes,*
> *and I shall keep it to the end.*
> Psalm 119:33 NKJV

As the first community to which a person is attached and the first authority under which a person learns to live, the family establishes society's most basic values.

Charles Colson

MORE WORDS FROM GOD'S WORD

For it is God who is working among you both the willing and the working for His good purpose.

Philippians 2:13 Holman CSB

Do what is right and good in the Lord's sight, so that you may prosper and so that you may enter and possess the good land the Lord your God swore to [give] your fathers.

Deuteronomy 6:18 Holman CSB

You will know the truth, and the truth will set you free.

John 8:32 Holman CSB

God's Way is not a matter of mere talk; it's an empowered life.

1 Corinthians 4:20 MSG

My Priorities for Life

I will focus my thoughts and energies on living a principled life.

I will study God's Word and do my best to live according to God's commandments.

I will seek to share my value system with family and friends.

Check Your Priority		
High	Med.	Low
—	—	—
—	—	—
—	—	—

Sensing God's Presence

You will seek Me and find Me when you search
for Me with all your heart.

Jeremiah 29:13 Holman CSB

In the quiet early morning, as the sun's first rays stream over the horizon, we may sense the presence of God. But as the day wears on and the demands of everyday life bear down upon us, we may become so wrapped up in earthy concerns that we forget to praise the Creator.

God is everywhere we have ever been and everywhere we will ever be. When we turn to Him often, we are blessed by His presence. But, if we ignore God's presence or rebel against it altogether, the world in which we live soon becomes a spiritual wasteland.

Since God is everywhere, we are free to sense His presence whenever we take the time to quiet our souls and turn our prayers to Him. But sometimes, amid the incessant demands of everyday life, we turn our thoughts far from God; when we do, we suffer.

Do you set aside quiet moments each day to offer praise to your Creator? You should. During these moments of stillness, you can sense the infinite love and power of our Lord. The familiar words of Psalm 46:10 remind us to "Be still, and know that I am God" (KJV). When we do so, we encounter the awesome presence of our loving Heavenly Father.

Are you tired, discouraged or fearful? Be comforted because God is with you. Are you confused? Listen to the quiet voice of your Heavenly Father. Are you bitter? Talk with God and seek His guidance. Are you celebrating a great victory? Thank God and praise Him. He is the Giver of all things good. In whatever condition you find yourself—whether you are happy or sad, victorious or vanquished, troubled or triumphant—celebrate God's presence. And be comforted in the knowledge that God is not just near. He is here.

If you want to hear God's voice clearly and you are uncertain, then remain in His presence until He changes that uncertainty. Often, much can happen during this waiting for the Lord. Sometimes, He changes pride into humility, doubt into faith and peace.

Corrie ten Boom

PRIORITIES FOR MY LIFE

Having trouble hearing God? If so, slow yourself down, tune out the distractions, and listen carefully. God has important things to say; your task is to be still and listen.

TIMELESS WISDOM FOR GODLY LIVING

He is more within us than we are ourselves.

Elizabeth Ann Seton

Make the least of all that goes and the most of all that comes. Don't regret what is past. Cherish what you have. Look forward to all that is to come. And most important of all, rely moment by moment on Jesus Christ.

Gigi Graham Tchividjian

God walks with us. He scoops us up in His arms or simply sits with us in silent strength until we cannot avoid the awesome recognition that yes, even now, He is here.

Gloria Gaither

In the sanctuary, we discover beauty: the beauty of His presence.

Kay Arthur

The Lord is near all who call out to Him, all who call out to Him with integrity. He fulfills the desires of those who fear Him; He hears their cry for help and saves them.
Psalm 145:18-19 Holman CSB

Sometimes the loveliness of God's presence comes in the midst of pain.

Madeleine L'Engle

MORE WORDS FROM GOD'S WORD

Surely goodness and mercy shall follow me all the days of my life: and I will dwell in the house of the Lord for ever.

Psalm 23:6 KJV

Again, this is God's command: to believe in his personally named Son, Jesus Christ. He told us to love each other, in line with the original command. As we keep his commands, we live deeply and surely in him, and he lives in us. And this is how we experience his deep and abiding presence in us: by the Spirit he gave us.

1 John 3:23-24 MSG

For the eyes of the Lord range throughout the earth to strengthen those whose hearts are fully committed to him.

2 Chronicles 16:9 NIV

My Priorities for Life

I believe God seeks a close and intimate relationship with me.

I believe that whenever I feel distance from God, that distance is my own doing, not His.

I believe God is near and that He is guiding me as I seek His wisdom.

Check Your Priority		
High	Med.	Low
—	—	—
—	—	—
—	—	—

Walking the Christian Path

Make it your ambition to lead a quiet life,
to mind your own business and to work with your hands, just as we told
you, so that your daily life may win the respect of outsiders
and so that you will not be dependent on anybody.

1 Thessalonians 4:11-12 NIV

God has given you the gift of life. How will you use that gift? Will you treat this day as a precious treasure from your Heavenly Father, or will you take the next 24 hours for granted? The answer should be obvious: Every day, including this one, comes gift-wrapped from God—your job is unwrap that gift, to use it wisely, and to give thanks to the Giver.

As anyone past the age of 40 can attest, life is shockingly brief. Time is, indeed, a nonrenewable resource, but sometimes, we fail to treat it that way. Instead of savoring each moment, we fall prey to the twin evils of pessimism and boredom. Instead of pursuing our highest priorities, we waste large quantities of time in trivial pursuits and petty diversions. Instead of treating each day as a cause for celebration, we wander from dawn to dusk, scarcely offering a single word of thanks to our Creator. And we suffer because of our shortsightedness.

Instead of sleepwalking through life, we must wake up and live in the precious present. Each waking moment holds the potential to celebrate, to serve, to share, or to love. Because we are beings with incalculable potential, each moment has incalculable value. Our challenge is to experience each day to the fullest as we seek to live in accordance with God's plan for our lives. When we do, we experience His abundance and His peace.

Are you willing to treat this day (and every one hereafter) as a special gift to be savored and celebrated? You should—and if you seek to Live with a capital L, you most certainly will.

Life is not a journey you want to make on autopilot.

Paula Rinehart

PRIORITIES FOR MY LIFE

Life is a priceless gift from God. Spend time each day thanking God for His gift.

TIMELESS WISDOM FOR GODLY LIVING

I've finally realized that if something has no significant value, it doesn't deserve my time. Life is not a dress rehearsal, and I'll never get this day again.

Sheri Rose Shepherd

To be human is to be fallible, but it is also to be capable of love and to be able to retain that childlike openness which enables us to go bravely into the darkness and towards that life of love and truth which will set us free.

Madeleine L'Engle

Not every day of our lives is overflowing with joy and celebration. But there are moments when our hearts nearly burst within us for the sheer joy of being alive. The first sight of our newborn babies, the warmth of love in another's eyes, the fresh scent of rain on a hot summer's eve—moments like these renew in us a heartfelt appreciation for life.

Gwen Ellis

I came so they can have real and eternal life, more and better life than they ever dreamed of.
John 10:10 MSG

A life lived without reflection can be very superficial and empty.

Elisabeth Elliot

MORE WORDS FROM GOD'S WORD

This day I call heaven and earth as witnesses against you that I have set before you life and death, blessings and curses. Now choose life, so that you and your children may live and that you may love the LORD your God, listen to his voice, and hold fast to him. For the LORD is your life, and he will give you many years in the land he swore to give to your fathers, Abraham, Isaac and Jacob.

Deuteronomy 30:19 NIV

I urge you to live a life worthy of the calling you have received.

Ephesians 4:1 NIV

I am the way and the truth and the life. No one comes to the Father except through me.

John 14:6 NIV

My Priorities for Life

	Check Your Priority	
	High Med. Low	

I consider my life to be a priceless gift from God.

—   —   —

I understand the importance of spending time each day thanking God for His blessings.

—   —   —

I slow down to marvel at the beauty of God's glorious creation.

—   —   —

I strive to make every day a cause for celebration.

—   —   —

The Ultimate Friend

And Jesus said to them,
"I am the bread of life. He who comes to Me shall never hunger,
and he who believes in Me shall never thirst."

John 6:35 NKJV

He was the Son of God, but He wore a crown of thorns. He was the Savior of mankind, yet He was put to death on a rough-hewn cross. He offered His healing touch to an unsaved world, and yet the same hands that had healed the sick and raised the dead were pierced with nails.

Jesus Christ, the Son of God, was born into humble circumstances. He walked this earth, not as a ruler of men, but as the Savior of mankind. His crucifixion, a torturous punishment that was intended to end His life and His reign, instead became the pivotal event in the history of all humanity. Christ sacrificed His life on the cross so that we might have eternal life. This gift, freely given by God's only begotten Son, is the priceless possession of everyone who accepts Him as Lord and Savior.

Why did Christ endure the humiliation and torture of the cross? He did it for you. His love is as near as your next breath, as personal as your next thought, more essential than your next heartbeat. And what must you do in response to the Savior's gifts? You must accept His love, praise His name, and share His message of salvation. And, you must conduct yourself in a manner that demonstrates to all the world that your acquaintance with the Master is not a passing fancy but that it is, instead, the cornerstone and the touchstone of your life.

In your greatest weakness, turn to your greatest strength, Jesus, and hear Him say, "My grace is sufficient for you, for My strength is made perfect in weakness" (2 Corinthians 12:9, NKJV).

Lisa Whelchel

For the Son of Man has come to save that which was lost.

Matthew 18:11 NKJV

PRIORITIES FOR MY LIFE

What a friend you have in Jesus! Jesus loves you, and He offers you eternal life with Him in heaven. Welcome Him into your heart. Now!

TIMELESS WISDOM FOR GODLY LIVING

Christians see sin for what it is: willful rebellion against the rulership of God in their lives. And in turning from their sin, they have embraced God's only means of dealing with sin: Jesus.

Kay Arthur

The crucial question for each of us is this: What do you think of Jesus, and do you yet have a personal acquaintance with Him?

Hannah Whitall Smith

When we are in a situation where Jesus is all we have, we soon discover he is all we really need.

Gigi Graham Tchividjian

At the name of Jesus every knee should bow, of those in heaven, and of those on earth, and of those under the earth, and that every tongue should confess that Jesus Christ is Lord, to the glory of God the Father.
Philippians 2:10-11 NKJV

To God be the glory, great things He has done; So loved He the world that He gave us His Son.

Fanny Crosby

MORE WORDS FROM GOD'S WORD

For I am persuaded, that neither death, nor life, nor angels, nor principalities, nor powers, nor things present, nor things to come, nor height, nor depth, nor any other creature, shall be able to separate us from the love of God, which is in Christ Jesus our Lord.

Romans 8:38-39 KJV

"For Jesus is the one referred to in the Scriptures, where it says, 'The stone that you builders rejected has now become the cornerstone.' There is salvation in no one else! There is no other name in all of heaven for people to call on to save them."

Acts 4:11-12 NLT

My Priorities for Life

I will accept Jesus as my personal Savior, and I will allow Him to reign over my heart.

I will share the Good News of Jesus with a world that desperately needs His message.

I will conduct myself in ways that clearly demonstrate the changes that Christ has made in my life.

I will make Jesus the cornerstone of my life, and I will honor Him today, tomorrow, and forever.

Check Your Priority		
High	Med.	Low
—	—	—
—	—	—
—	—	—
—	—	—

Loving and Obeying God

It is the LORD your God you must follow,
and him you must revere. Keep his commands and obey him;
serve him and hold fast to him.

Deuteronomy 13:4 NIV

Obedience to God is determined, not by words, but by deeds. Talking about righteousness is easy; living righteously is far more difficult, especially in today's temptation-filled world.

Since God created Adam and Eve, we human beings have been rebelling against our Creator. Why? Because we are unwilling to trust God's Word, and we are unwilling to follow His commandments. God has given us a guidebook for righteous living called the Holy Bible. It contains thorough instructions which, if followed, lead to fulfillment, abundance, and salvation. But, if we choose to ignore God's commandments, the results are as predictable as they are tragic.

In Ephesians 2:10 we read, "For we are His workmanship, created in Christ Jesus for good works." (NKJV). These words are instructive: We are not saved by good works, but for good works. Good works are not the root, but rather the fruit of our salvation.

When we seek righteousness in our own lives—and when we seek the companionship of those who do likewise—we reap the spiritual rewards that God intends for our lives. When we behave ourselves as godly men and women, we honor God. When we live righteously and according to God's commandments, He blesses us in ways that we cannot fully understand.

Do you seek God's peace and His blessings? Then obey Him. When you're faced with a difficult choice or a powerful temptation, seek God's counsel and trust the counsel He gives. Invite God into your heart and live according to His commandments. When you do, you will be blessed today, and tomorrow, and forever.

God is God. Because He is God, He is worthy of my trust and obedience. I will find rest nowhere but in His holy will, a will that is unspeakably beyond my largest notions of what He is up to.

Elisabeth Elliot

PRIORITIES FOR MY LIFE

Obedience leads to spiritual growth: Anne Graham Lotz correctly observed, "If you want to discover your spiritual gifts, start obeying God. As you serve Him, you will find that He has given you the gifts that are necessary to follow through in obedience."

TIMELESS WISDOM FOR GODLY LIVING

The pathway of obedience can sometimes be difficult, but it always leads to a strengthening of our inner woman.

Vonette Bright

I know the power obedience has for making things easy which seem impossible.

St. Teresa of Avila

Obedience goes before our hearts and carries them where they would not normally go.

Paula Rinehart

God asked both Noah and Joshua to do something unusual and difficult. They did it, and their obedience brought them deliverance.

Mary Morrison Suggs

The world and its desires pass away,
but the man who does the will of God lives forever.
1 John 2:17 NIV

Rejoicing is a matter of obedience to God—an obedience that will start you on the road to peace and contentment.

Kay Arthur

MORE WORDS FROM GOD'S WORD

So roll up your sleeves, put your mind in gear, be totally ready to receive the gift that's coming when Jesus arrives. Don't lazily slip back into those old grooves of evil, doing just what you feel like doing. You didn't know any better then; you do now. As obedient children, let yourselves be pulled into a way of life shaped by God's life, a life energetic and blazing with holiness.

1 Peter 1:13-15 MSG

If they obey and serve him, they will spend the rest of their days in prosperity and their years in contentment.

Job 36:11 NIV

For it is not those who hear the law who are righteous in God's sight, but it is those who obey the law who will be declared righteous.

Romans 2:13 NIV

My Priorities for Life

I understand that my obedience to God is a demonstration of the gratitude that I feel in my heart for the blessings I have been given.

When I obey God, I feel better about myself.

Obedience to God may not always be easy or pleasant, but it is always satisfying.

Check Your Priority		
High	Med.	Low
—	—	—
—	—	—
—	—	—

The Joys of Friendship

Greater love has no one than this,
that he lay down his life for his friends.

John 15:13 NIV

Some friendships help us honor God; these friendships should be nurtured. Other friendships place us in situations where we are tempted to dishonor God by disobeying His commandments; friendships such as these have the potential to do us great harm.

Because we tend to become like our friends, we must choose our friends carefully. Because our friends influence us in ways that are both subtle and powerful, we must ensure that our friendships are pleasing to God. When we spend our days in the presence of godly believers, we are blessed, not only by those friends, but also by our Creator.

Do you spend time with people who make you a better Christian, or are you spending time with people who encourage you to stray from your faith? The answer to this question will have a surprising impact on the condition of your spiritual health. Why? Because our friends help shape our lives and our attitudes. So, one of the best ways to ensure that you follow Christ is to find fellow believers who are willing to follow Him with you.

Many elements of society seek to mold you into a more worldly being; God, on the other hand, seeks to mold you into a new being, a new creation through Christ, a being that is most certainly not conformed to this world. If you are to please God, you must resist the pressures that society seeks to impose upon you, and you must choose, instead, to follow in the footsteps of His only begotten Son.

Inasmuch as anyone pushes you nearer to God,
he or she is your friend.

Barbara Johnson

You could have been born in another time and another place,
but God determined to "people" your life
with these particular friends.

Joni Eareckson Tada

PRIORITIES FOR MY LIFE

If you're trying to make new friends, become interested in them
. . . and eventually they'll become interested in you.

TIMELESS WISDOM FOR GODLY LIVING

We long to find someone who has been where we've been, who shares our fragile skies, who sees our sunsets with the same shades of blue.

Beth Moore

My special friends, who know me so well and love me anyway, give me daily encouragement to keep on.

Emilie Barnes

The best times in life are made a thousand times better when shared with a dear friend.

Luci Swindoll

A friend loves you all the time,
and a brother helps in time of trouble.
Proverbs 17:17 NCV

We are indeed rich when we have many friends, and I am thoroughly convinced that God loves us, encourages us, nurtures us, and supports us through other human beings.

Marilyn Meberg

MORE WORDS FROM GOD'S WORD

As iron sharpens iron, a friend sharpens a friend.

Proverbs 27:17 NLT

If a fellow believer hurts you, go and tell him—work it out between the two of you. If he listens, you've made a friend.

Matthew 18:15 MSG

Beloved, if God so loved us, we also ought to love one another.

1 John 4:11 NKJV

Iron sharpeneth iron; so a man sharpeneth the countenance of his friend.

Proverbs 27:17 KJV

Finally, all of you be of one mind, having compassion for one another; love as brothers, be tenderhearted, be courteous.

1 Peter 3:8 NKJV

My Priorities for Life

I value close friendships . . .

I understand that lasting friendships are built upon a foundation of honesty, kindness, and mutual trust.

Because I want to cultivate my friendships, I make the effort to spend time with my friends.

Check Your Priority		
High	Med.	Low
—	—	—.
—	—	—
—	—	—

Real Prosperity

For I am the Lord, I do not change. Will a man rob God?
Yet you have robbed Me! But you say, in what way have we robbed You?
In tithes and offerings. You are cursed with a curse, for you have robbed
Me, even this whole nation. Bring all the tithes into the storehouse,
that there may be food in My house.

Malachi 3:6, 8-10 NKJV

Sometimes, our financial struggles are simply manifestations of the inner conflict that we feel when we stray from God's path. The beautiful words of John 14:27 remind us that Jesus offers us peace, not as the world gives, but as He alone gives. Our challenge is to accept Christ's peace into our hearts and then, as best we can, to share His peace with our families and friends.

When we summon the courage and the determination to implement a sensible financial plan, we invite peace into our lives. But, we should never confuse earthly peace (with a small "p") with spiritual Peace (the heavenly Peace—with a capital "P"— that flows from the Prince of Peace).

When we accept Jesus as our personal Savior, we are transformed by His grace. We are then free to accept the spiritual abundance and peace that can be ours through the power of the risen Christ.

Have you found the genuine peace that can be yours through Christ? Or are you still rushing after the illusion of "peace and happiness" that the world promises but cannot deliver? Today, as a gift to yourself and to your loved ones, claim the inner peace that is your spiritual birthright: the peace of Jesus Christ. It is offered freely; it has been paid for in full; it is yours for the asking. So ask. And then share.

Financial peace can, and should, be yours. But the spiritual peace that stems from your personal relationship with Jesus must be yours if you are to receive the eternal abundance of our Lord. Claim that abundance today.

If the Living Logos of God has the power to create and sustain the universe . . . . He is more than able to sustain your marriage and your ministry, your faith and your finances, your hope and your health.

Anne Graham Lotz

PRIORITIES FOR MY LIFE

Don't fall in love with "stuff." We live in a society that worships "stuff"—don't fall into that trap. Remember this: "stuff" is highly overrated. Worship God Almighty, not the almighty dollar.

TIMELESS WISDOM FOR GODLY LIVING

Here's a good recipe for managing your money: Never make a big financial decision without first talking it over with God.

Marie T. Freeman

Christians cannot experience peace in the area of finances until they have surrendered total control of this area to God and accepted their position as stewards.

Larry Burkett

If your outgo exceeds your income, then your upkeep will be your downfall.

John Maxwell

The best money advice I ever got was from my father. He said, "Don't spend anything unless you have to."

Dinah Shore

And my God shall supply all your need according to His riches in glory by Christ Jesus.
Philippians 4:19 NKJV

Money separates people more often than it joins them.

Liz Curtis Higgs

MORE WORDS FROM GOD'S WORD

Honor the Lord with your wealth and the firstfruits from all your crops. Then your barns will be full, and your wine barrels will overflow with new wine.

Proverbs 3:9-10 NCV

Then she came and told the man of God. And he said, "Go, sell the oil and pay your debt; and you and your sons live on the rest."

2 Kings 4:7 NKJV

Based on the gift they have received, everyone should use it to serve others, as good managers of the varied grace of God.

1 Peter 4:10 Holman CSB

My Priorities for Life

God is my ultimate financial advisor. I will trust Him with everything I have.

I understand the importance of being a careful steward of the money that God has entrusted to my care.

I will be generous with my tithes and offerings because I understand that everything I have ultimately belongs to God.

Check Your Priority		
High	Med.	Low
—	—	—
—	—	—
—	—	—

The Power of Encouragement

So encourage each other and give each other strength,
just as you are doing now.

1 Thessalonians 5:11 NCV

Life is a team sport, and all of us need occasional pats on the back from our teammates. This world can be a difficult place, a place where many of our friends and family members are troubled by the challenges of everyday life. And since we cannot always be certain who needs our help, we should strive to speak helpful words to all who cross our paths.

In his letter to the Ephesians, Paul writes, "Do not let any unwholesome talk come out of your mouths, but only what is helpful for building others up according to their needs, that it may benefit those who listen" (v. 29 NIV). This passage reminds us that, as Christians, we are instructed to choose our words carefully so as to build others up through wholesome, honest encouragement. How can we build others up? By celebrating their victories and their accomplishments. As the old saying goes, "When someone does something good, applaud—you'll make two people happy."

Genuine encouragement should never be confused with pity. God intends for His children to lead lives of abundance, joy, celebration and praise—not lives of self-pity or regret. So we must guard ourselves against hosting (or joining) the "pity parties" that so often accompany difficult times. Instead, we must encourage each other to have faith—first in God and His only begotten Son—and then in our own abilities to use the talents God has given us for the furtherance of His kingdom and for the betterment of our own lives.

As a faithful follower of Jesus, you have every reason to be hopeful, and you have every reason to share your hopes with others. When you do, you will discover that hope, like other human emotions, is contagious. So do the world (and yourself) a favor: Look for the good in others and celebrate the good that you find. When you do, you'll be a powerful force of encouragement to your friends and family . . . and a worthy servant to your God.

We do have the ability to encourage or discourage each other with the words we say. In order to maintain a positive mood, our hearts must be in good condition.

Annie Chapman

PRIORITIES FOR MY LIFE

Be a booster, not a cynic. Cynicism is contagious, and so is optimism. Think and act accordingly.

TIMELESS WISDOM FOR GODLY LIVING

Sometimes one little spark of kindness is all it takes to reignite the light of hope in a heart that's blinded by pain.

Barbara Johnson

A single word, if spoken in a friendly spirit, may be sufficient to turn one from dangerous error.

Fanny Crosby

So often we think that to be encouragers we have to produce great words of wisdom when, in fact, a few simple syllables of sympathy and an arm around the shoulder can often provide much needed comfort.

Florence Littauer

He comes alongside us when we go through hard times, and before you know it, he brings us alongside someone else who is going through hard times so that we can be there for that person just as God was there for us.

2 Corinthians 1:4 MSG

Words. Do you fully understand their power? Can any of us really grasp the mighty force behind the things we say? Do we stop and think before we speak, considering the potency of the words we utter?

Joni Eareckson Tada

MORE WORDS FROM GOD'S WORD

Encourage each other. Live in harmony and peace. Then the God of love and peace will be with you.

2 Corinthians 13:11 NLT

So don't lose a minute in building on what you've been given, complementing your basic faith with good character, spiritual understanding, alert discipline, passionate patience, reverent wonder, warm friendliness, and generous love, each dimension fitting into and developing the others.

2 Peter 1:5-7 MSG

But encourage one another day after day, as long as it is still called "Today," so that none of you will be hardened by the deceitfulness of sin.

Hebrews 3:13 NASB

My Priorities for Life

I believe that God wants me to encourage others.

I carefully think about the words I speak so that every word might be a "gift of encouragement" to others.

My words reflect my heart. I will guard my heart so that my words will be pleasing to God.

| Check Your Priority | | |
High	Med.	Low
—	—	—
—	—	—
—	—	—

Beginning the Day with God

He awakens Me morning by morning, He awakens My ear to hear as the learned. The Lord God has opened My ear.

Isaiah 50:4-5 NKJV

Does God come first in your life and your day? Hopefully so. When Jesus was tempted by Satan, the Master's response was unambiguous. Jesus chose to worship the Lord and "serve Him only" (Matthew 4:10 Holman CSB). We, as believers in Christ, must follow in His footsteps by placing God first.

When we mistakenly place God in a position of secondary importance, we do ourselves great harm. When we allow the obligations of everyday life to come between us and our Creator, we suffer. But, when we imitate Jesus and place the Lord in His rightful place—at the center of our lives—then we claim spiritual treasures that will endure forever.

When we begin each day with heads bowed and hearts lifted, we remind ourselves of God's love, His protection, and His commandments. And if we are wise, we align our priorities for the coming day with the teachings and commandments that God has given us through His Holy Word.

Are you if the habit of talking to your Creator each morning? If so, you're to be congratulated. There's no better way to start your day than with a steaming cup of coffee and a heartfelt conversation with God.

Every day has its own particular brand of holiness to discover and worship appropriately.

Annie Dillard

But seek first the kingdom of God and His righteousness, and all these things shall be added to you.

Matthew 6:33 NKJV

PRIORITIES FOR MY LIFE

Decide how much of your time God deserves, and then give it to Him. Don't organize your day so that God gets "what's left." Give Him what you honestly believe He deserves.

TIMELESS WISDOM FOR GODLY LIVING

I think that God required the Israelites to gather manna every morning so that they would learn to come to Him daily.

Cynthia Heald

Faithful prayer warriors and devoted Bible lovers will tell you that their passion for disciplined quiet time with the Lord is not a sign of strength but an admission of weakness—a hard-earned realization that they are nothing on their own compared with who they are after they've been with him.

Doris Greig

Every morning is a fresh opportunity to find God's extraordinary joy in the most ordinary places.

Janet. L. Weaver

A quiet morning with a loving God puts the events of the upcoming day into proper perspective.

Janette Oke

It is good to give thanks to the Lord, to sing praises to the Most High. It is good to proclaim your unfailing love in the morning, your faithfulness in the evening.

Psalm 92:1-2 NLT

God calls us to seek him daily in order to serve him daily.

Sheila Cragg

MORE WORDS FROM GOD'S WORD

Truly my soul silently waits for God; from Him comes my salvation.

Psalm 62:1 NKJV

May the words of my mouth and the thoughts of my heart be pleasing to you, O Lord, my rock and my redeemer.

Psalm 19:14 NLT

Be still, and know that I am God.

Psalm 46:10 NKJV

But grow in the grace and knowledge of our Lord and Savior Jesus Christ. To Him be the glory both now and to the day of eternity.

2 Peter 3:18 Holman CSB

My Priorities for Life

I understand the importance of spending time each day with God.

I have a regular time and place where I can read, pray, and talk to God.

I try to listen carefully to the things that God places upon my heart.

Check Your Priority		
High	Med.	Low
—	—	—
—	—	—
—	—	—

Claiming Contentment in a Discontented World

But godliness with contentment is great gain. For we brought
nothing into the world, and we can take nothing out of it.
But if we have food and clothing, we will be content with that.

1 Timothy 6:6-8 NIV

When we conduct ourselves in ways that are opposed to God's commandments, we rob ourselves of God's peace. When we fall prey to the temptations and distractions of our irreverent age, we rob ourselves of God's blessings. When we become preoccupied with material possessions or personal status, we forfeit the contentment that is rightfully ours in Christ.

Where can we find the kind of contentment that Paul describes in Philippians 4? Is it a result of wealth, or power, or fame? Hardly. Genuine contentment is a gift from God to those who follow His commandments and accept His Son. When Christ dwells at the center of our families and our lives, contentment will belong to us just as surely as we belong to Him.

Do you seek happiness, abundance, and contentment? If so, here are some things you should do: Love God and His Son; depend upon God for strength; try, to the best of your abilities, to follow God's will; and strive to obey His Holy Word. When you do these things, you'll discover that happiness goes hand-in-hand with righteousness. The happiest people are not those who rebel against God; the happiest people are those who love God and obey His commandments.

What does life have in store for you? A world full of possibilities (of course it's up to you to seize them), and God's promise of abundance (of course it's up to you to accept it). So, as you embark upon the next phase of your journey, remember to celebrate the life that God has given you. Your Creator has blessed you beyond measure. Honor Him with your prayers, your words, your deeds, and your joy.

Are you a contented Christian? If so, then you are well aware of the healing power of the risen Christ. But if your spirit is temporarily troubled, perhaps you need to focus less upon your own priorities and more upon God's priorities. When you do, you'll rediscover this life-changing truth: Genuine contentment begins with God . . . and ends there.

PRIORITIES FOR MY LIFE

Be contented where you are, even if it's not exactly where you want to end up: Think about it like this: God has something wonderful in store for you—and remember that God's timing is perfect—so be patient, trust God, do your best, and expect the best.

TIMELESS WISDOM FOR GODLY LIVING

If God chooses to remain silent, faith is content.

Ruth Bell Graham

If I could just hang in there, being faithful to my own tasks, God would make me joyful and content. The responsibility is mine, but the power is His.

Peg Rankin

The key to contentment is to consider. Consider who you are and be satisfied with that. Consider what you have and be satisfied with that. Consider what God's doing and be satisfied with that.

Luci Swindoll

Let your character be free from the love of money, being content with what you have; for He Himself has said, "I will never desert you, nor will I ever forsake you."

Hebrews 13:5 NASB

Father and Mother lived on the edge of poverty, and yet their contentment was not dependent upon their surroundings. Their relationship to each other and to the Lord gave them strength and happiness.

Corrie ten Boom

MORE WORDS FROM GOD'S WORD

I've learned by now to be quite content whatever my circumstances. I'm just as happy with little as with much, with much as with little. I've found the recipe for being happy whether full or hungry, hands full or hands empty.

Philippians 4:11-12 MSG

A tranquil heart is life to the body, but jealousy is rottenness to the bones.
Proverbs 14:30 Holman CSB

Because your love is better than life, my lips will glorify you. I will praise you as long as I live, and in your name I will lift up my hands. My soul will be satisfied as with the richest of foods; with singing lips my mouth will praise you.

Psalm 63:3-5 NIV

My Priorities for Life

I believe that peace with God is the starting point for a contented life.

Check Your Priority		
High	Med.	Low
—	—	—

I understand that contentment comes, not from my circumstances, but from my attitude.

—	—	—

I understand that one way to find contentment is to praise God continually and thank Him for His blessings.

—	—	—

God's Wisdom

The Lord says,
"I will make you wise and show you where to go.
I will guide you and watch over you."

Psalm 32:8 NCV

If we call upon our Lord, if we study His teachings, and if we seek to see the world through His eyes, He gives us guidance, wisdom and perspective. When we make God's priorities our priorities, He leads us according to His plan and according to His commandments. When we study God's Word, we are reminded that God's reality is the ultimate reality. But sometimes, when the demands of the day threaten to overwhelm us, we lose perspective, and we forfeit the blessings that God bestows upon those who accept His wisdom and His peace.

Do you seek to live according to God's plan? If so, you must study His Word. You must seek out worthy teachers and listen carefully to their advice. You must associate, day in and day out, with godly men and women. And then, as you accumulate wisdom, you must not keep it for yourself; you must, instead, share it with others.

But be forewarned: if you sincerely seek to share your hard-earned wisdom with the world, your actions must give credence to your words. The best way to share one's wisdom—perhaps the only way—is not by proclamation, but by example.

Are you a woman who embraces God's wisdom? And do you apply that wisdom to every aspect of your life? If so, you will be blessed by Him . . . today, tomorrow, and forever.

Wisdom enlarges our capacity for discovery and delight,
causing wonder to grow as we grow.

Susan Lenzkes

Let the word of Christ dwell in you richly in all wisdom;
teaching and admonishing one another in psalms
and hymns and spiritual songs, singing with grace
in your hearts to the Lord.

Colossians 3:16 KJV

PRIORITIES FOR MY LIFE

Need wisdom? God's got it. If you want it, then study God's Word and associate with godly people.

TIMELESS WISDOM FOR GODLY LIVING

Knowledge can be learned, but wisdom must be earned. Wisdom is knowledge . . . lived.

Sheila Walsh

Knowledge can be found in books or in school. Wisdom, on the other hand, starts with God . . . and ends there.

Marie T. Freeman

Wisdom always waits for the right time to act, while emotion always pushes for action right now.

Joyce Meyer

Our first step toward gaining God's wisdom is to know what we do not know; that is, to be aware of our shortcomings.

Dianna Booher

Wisdom is the principal thing; therefore get wisdom. And in all your getting, get understanding.
Proverbs 4:7 NKJV

Wisdom is knowledge applied. Head knowledge is useless on the battlefield. Knowledge stamped on the heart makes one wise.

Beth Moore

MORE WORDS FROM GOD'S WORD

Happy is the person who finds wisdom, the one who gets understanding.

Proverbs 3:13 NCV

Anyone who listens to my teaching and obeys me is wise, like a person who builds a house on solid rock. Though the rain comes in torrents and the floodwaters rise and the winds beat against that house, it won't collapse, because it is built on rock.

Matthew 7:24–25 NLT

But the wisdom that is from above is first pure, then peaceable, gentle, willing to yield, full of mercy and good fruits, without partiality and without hypocrisy.

James 3:17 NKJV

My Priorities for Life

I will continually remind myself of God's wisdom by reading the Bible each day.

I will do my best to live wisely by obeying the teachings that I find in God's Word.

I will share my wisdom with friends and family members who seek my advice.

I will associate with wise men and wise women.

Check Your Priority		
High	Med.	Low
—	—	—
—	—	—
—	—	—
—	—	—

Sharing Your Testimony

Therefore, everyone who will acknowledge Me before men,
I will also acknowledge him before My Father in heaven.

Matthew 10:32 Holman CSB

Have you made the decision to allow Christ to reign over your heart? If so, you have an important story to tell: yours.

Your personal testimony is profoundly important, but perhaps because of shyness (or because of the fear of being rebuffed), you've been hesitant to share your experiences. If so, you should start paying less attention to your own insecurities and more attention to the message that God wants you to share with the world.

In his second letter to Timothy, Paul shares a message to believers of every generation when he writes, "God has not given us a spirit of timidity" (1:7 NASB). Paul's meaning is clear: When sharing our testimonies, we must be courageous, forthright, and unashamed.

Corrie ten Boom observed, "There is nothing anybody else can do that can stop God from using us. We can turn everything into a testimony." Her words remind us that when we speak up for God, our actions may speak even more loudly than our words.

When we let other people know the details of our faith, we assume an important responsibility: the responsibility of making certain that our words are reinforced by our actions. When we share our testimonies, we must also be willing to serve as shining examples of righteousness—undeniable examples of the changes that Jesus makes in the lives of those who accept Him as their Savior.

Are you willing to follow in the footsteps of Jesus? If so, you must also be willing to talk about Him. And make no mistake—the time to express your belief in Him is now. You know how He has touched your own heart; help Him do the same for others.

I love to tell the story of unseen things above,
of Jesus and His Glory, of Jesus and His love.

A. Catherine Hankey

PRIORITIES FOR MY LIFE

If your eternity with God is secure (because you believe in Jesus), you have a profound responsibility to tell as many people as you can about the eternal life that Christ offers to those who believe in Him.

TIMELESS WISDOM FOR GODLY LIVING

My personal experience is often more acceptable to an unbeliever or skeptic than any historical facts and evidences that I could rattle off.

Becky Tirabassi

Those who are not yet in the family of Christ need us to be his hands, his feet, his eyes, his ears, and his voice to help them find God's love.

Doris Greig

Claim the joy that is yours. Pray. And know that your joy is used by God to reach others.

Kay Arthur

But the following night the Lord stood by him and said, "Be of good cheer, Paul; for as you have testified for Me."
Acts 23:11 NKJV

Faith in small things has repercussions that ripple all the way out. In a huge, dark room a little match can light up the place.

Joni Eareckson Tada

MORE WORDS FROM GOD'S WORD

This and this only has been my appointed work: getting this news to those who have never heard of God, and explaining how it works by simple faith and plain truth.

1 Timothy 2:7 MSG

For God has not given us a spirit of fear and timidity, but of power, love, and self-discipline. So you must never be ashamed to tell others about our Lord.

2 Timothy 1:7-8 NLT

But when the Holy Spirit has come upon you, you will receive power and will tell people about me everywhere—in Jerusalem, throughout Judea, in Samaria, and to the ends of the earth.

Acts 1:8 NLT

My Priorities for Life

I believe that it is important to share my testimony.

I feel that my actions are as much a part of my testimony as my words.

I feel that my testimony has the power to change the world.

	Check Your Priority	
High	Med.	Low
—	—	—
—	—	—
—	—	—

The Importance of Words

So then, rid yourselves of all evil, all lying, hypocrisy, jealousy,
and evil speech. As newborn babies want milk, you should want
the pure and simple teaching. By it you can grow up and be saved.

1 Peter 2:1–2 NCV

As you think about the day ahead, think about the quality and tone of the words you intend to speak. Hopefully, you understand that your words have great power . . . because they most certainly do. If your words are encouraging, you can lift others up; if your words are hurtful, you can hold others back.

The Bible makes it clear that " Careless words stab like a sword." So, if you hope to solve problems instead of starting them, you must measure your words carefully. But sometimes, you'll be tempted to speak first and think second (with decidedly mixed results).

When you're frustrated or tired, you may say things that would be better left unspoken. Whenever you lash out in anger, you forgo the wonderful opportunity to consider your thoughts before you give voice to them. When you speak impulsively, you may, quite unintentionally, injure others.

A far better strategy, of course, is to do the more difficult thing: to think first and to speak next. When you do so, you give yourself ample time to compose your thoughts and to consult your Creator (but not necessarily in that order!)

Do you seek to be the kind of woman who is a continuing source of encouragement to others? Do you want to be a beacon of hope to your friends and family? And, do you seek to be a worthy ambassador for Christ? If so, you must speak words that are worthy of your Savior. So avoid angry outbursts. Refrain from impulsive outpourings. Terminate tantrums. Instead, speak words of encouragement and hope to a world that desperately needs both.

We will always experience regret when we live
for the moment and do not weigh our
words and deeds before we give them life.

Lisa Bevere

PRIORITIES FOR MY LIFE

When in doubt, use the Golden Rule to help you decide what to say: If you wouldn't like it said about you, don't say it about them!

TIMELESS WISDOM FOR GODLY LIVING

Every word we speak, every action we take, has an effect on the totality of humanity. No one can escape that privilege—or that responsibility.

Laurie Beth Jones

The things that we feel most deeply we ought to learn to be silent about, at least until we have talked them over thoroughly with God.

Elisabeth Elliot

The battle of the tongue is won not in the mouth, but in the heart.

Annie Chapman

Be gracious in your speech. The goal is to bring out the best in others in a conversation, not put them down, not cut them out.
Colossians 4:6 MSG

Fill the heart with the love of Christ so that only truth and purity can come out of the mouth.

Warren Wiersbe

MORE WORDS FROM GOD'S WORD

To everything there is a season . . . a time to keep silence, and a time to speak.

Ecclesiastes 3:1,7 KJV

Watch the way you talk. Let nothing foul or dirty come out of your mouth. Say only what helps, each word a gift.

Ephesians 4:29 MSG

If anyone considers himself religious and yet does not keep a tight rein on his tongue, he deceives himself and his religion is worthless.

James 1:26 NIV

Avoid irreverent, empty speech, for this will produce an even greater measure of godlessness.

2 Timothy 2:16 Holman CSB

My Priorities for Life

Every day, I try to find at least one person to encourage.

I believe that my words are important, so I try to think before I speak, not after.

I find that when I encourage others, I too, am encouraged.

Check Your Priority		
High	Med.	Low
—	—	—
—	—	—
—	—	—

An Attitude That Is Pleasing to God

Set your mind on things above, not on things on the earth.

Colossians 3:2 NKJV

The Christian life is a cause for celebration, but sometimes we don't feel much like celebrating. In fact, when the weight of the world seems to bear down upon our shoulders, celebration may be the last thing on our minds . . . but it shouldn't be. As God's children, we are all blessed beyond measure on good days and bad. This day is a non-renewable resource—once it's gone, it's gone forever. We should give thanks for this day while using it for the glory of God.

What's your attitude today? Are you fearful, angry, bored, or worried? Are you pessimistic, perplexed, pained, and perturbed? Are you moping around with a frown on your face that's almost as big as the one in your heart? If so, God wants to have a little talk with you.

God created you in His own image, and He wants you to experience joy, contentment, peace, and abundance. But, God will not force you to experience these things; you must claim them for yourself.

God has given you free will, including the ability to influence the direction and the tone of your thoughts. And, here's how God wants you to direct those thoughts: "Finally brothers, whatever is true, whatever is honorable, whatever is just, whatever is pure, whatever is lovely, whatever is commendable—if there is any moral excellence and if there is any praise—dwell on these things" (Philippians 4:8 Holman CSB).

The quality of your attitude will help determine the quality of your life, so you must guard your thoughts accordingly. If you make up your mind to approach life with a healthy mixture of realism and optimism, you'll be rewarded. But, if you allow yourself to fall into the unfortunate habit of negative thinking, you will doom yourself to unhappiness, or mediocrity, or worse.

So, the next time you find yourself dwelling upon the negative aspects of your life, refocus your attention on positive things. The next time you find yourself falling prey to the blight of pessimism, stop yourself and turn your thoughts around. The next time you're tempted to waste valuable time gossiping or complaining, resist those temptations with all your might.

And remember: You'll never whine your way to the top . . . so don't waste your breath.

PRIORITIES FOR MY LIFE

Focus on possibilities, not stumbling blocks: Of course you will encounter occasional disappointments, and, from time to time, you will encounter failure. But, don't invest large amounts of energy focusing on past misfortunes. Instead, look to the future with optimism and hope.

TIMELESS WISDOM FOR GODLY LIVING

No matter how little we can change about our circumstances, we always have a choice about our attitude toward the situation.

Vonette Bright

Each one of us is responsible for our own happiness. If we choose to allow ourselves to become miserable and unhappy, the problem is ours, not someone else's.

Joyce Meyer

The things we think are the things that feed our souls. If we think on pure and lovely things, we shall grow pure and lovely like them; and the converse is equally true.

Hannah Whitall Smith

Attitude is the mind's paintbrush; it can color any situation.

Barbara Johnson

Come near to God, and God will come near to you.
You sinners, clean sin out of your lives.
You who are trying to follow God and the world
at the same time, make your thinking pure.
James 4:8 NCV

Some people complain that God put thorns on roses, while others praise Him for putting roses on thorns.

Anonymous

MORE WORDS FROM GOD'S WORD

Finally, brethren, whatever is true, whatever is honorable, whatever is right, whatever is pure, whatever is lovely, whatever is of good repute, if there is any excellence and if anything worthy of praise, dwell on these things.

Philippians 4:8 NASB

So prepare your minds for service and have self-control.

1 Peter 1:13 NCV

A miserable heart means a miserable life; a cheerful heart fills the day with a song.

Proverbs 15:15 MSG

My Priorities for Life

I believe that if I want to change certain aspects of my life, I also need to make adjustments in my own attitudes toward life.

I believe that it is important to associate myself with people who are upbeat, optimistic, and encouraging.

I believe that it is important to focus my thoughts on the positive aspects of life, not the negative ones.

Check Your Priority		
High	Med.	Low
—	—	—
—	—	—
—	—	—

Praise for the Father

Is anyone happy? Let him sing songs of praise.

James 5:13 NIV

It has been called the most widely-used book of the Old Testament; it is, of course, the book of Psalms. In the Hebrew version of the Old Testament, the title of the book is translated "Hymns of Praise," and with good reason. Much of the book is a breathtakingly beautiful celebration of God's power, God's love, and God's creation.

The psalmist writes, "Let everything that has breath praise the Lord. Praise the Lord" (150:6). As Christians, we should continually praise God for all that He has done and all that He will do. For believers who have accepted the transforming love of Jesus Christ, there is simply no other way.

When is the best time to praise God? In church? Before dinner is served? When we tuck little children into bed? None of the above. The best time to praise God is all day, every day, to the greatest extent we can, with thanksgiving in our hearts.

Mrs. Charles E. Cowman, the author of the classic devotional text, *Streams in the Desert*, wrote, "Two wings are necessary to lift our souls toward God: prayer and praise. Prayer asks. Praise accepts the answer." That's why we should find the time to lift our concerns to God in prayer, and to praise Him for all that He has done.

Today, as you travel to work or school, as you hug your child or kiss your spouse, as you gaze upon a passing cloud or marvel at a glorious sunset, think of what God has done for you, for yours, and for all of us. And, every time you notice a gift from the Giver of all things good, praise Him. His works are marvelous, His gifts are beyond understanding, and His love endures forever.

God is worthy of our praise and is pleased when we come before Him with thanksgiving.

Shirley Dobson

Praise him, all you people of the earth, for he loves us with unfailing love; the faithfulness of the Lord endures forever. Praise the Lord!

Psalm 117 NLT

PRIORITIES FOR MY LIFE

When you pray, don't just ask God for things—also take time to praise Him.

TIMELESS WISDOM FOR GODLY LIVING

May your life become one of glad and unending praise to the Lord as you journey through this world, and in the world that is to come!

St. Teresa of Avila

Nothing we do is more powerful or more life-changing than praising God.

Stormie Omartian

Praising God reduces your cares, levels your anxieties, and multiplies your blessings.

Suzanne Dale Ezell

He is exalted, the King is exalted on high; I will praise Him.

Twila Paris

Through Him then, let us continually offer up a sacrifice of praise to God, that is, the fruit of lips that give thanks to His name.
Hebrews 13:15 NASB

I am to praise God for all things, regardless of where they seem to originate. Doing this is the key to receiving the blessings of God. Praise will wash away my resentments.

Catherine Marshall

MORE WORDS FROM GOD'S WORD

The LORD is my strength and song, and He has become my salvation; He is my God, and I will praise Him.

Exodus 15:2 NIV

And suddenly there was with the angel a multitude of the heavenly host praising God and saying: "Glory to God in the highest, And on earth peace, goodwill toward men!"

Luke 2:13-14 NKJV

At the name of Jesus every knee should bow, of those in heaven, and of those on earth, and of those under the earth, and that every tongue should confess that Jesus Christ is Lord, to the glory of God the Father.

Philippians 2:10-11 NKJV

My Priorities for Life

	Check Your Priority	
High	Med.	Low

I understand that prayer strengthens my relationship with God.

— — —

I trust that God will care for me, even when it seems that my prayers have gone unanswered.

— — —

I believe that my prayers have the power to change my circumstances, my perspective, and my future.

— — —

Patience and Trust

Knowing God leads to self-control. Self-control leads to patient endurance, and patient endurance leads to godliness.

2 Peter 1:6 NLT

The dictionary defines the word patience as "the ability to be calm, tolerant, and understanding." If that describes you, you can skip the rest of this page. But, if you're like most of us, you'd better keep reading.

For most of us, patience is a hard thing to master. Why? Because we have lots of things we want, and we know precisely when we want them: NOW (if not sooner). But our Father in heaven has other ideas; the Bible teaches that we must learn to wait patiently for the things that God has in store for us, even when waiting is difficult.

We live in an imperfect world inhabited by imperfect people. Sometimes, we inherit troubles from others, and sometimes we create troubles for ourselves. On other occasions, we see other people "moving ahead" in the world, and we want to move ahead with them. So we become impatient with ourselves, with our circumstances, and even with our Creator.

Psalm 37:7 commands us to "rest in the Lord, and wait patiently for Him" (NKJV). But, for most of us, waiting patiently for Him is hard. We are fallible human beings who seek solutions to our problems today, not tomorrow. Still, God instructs us to wait patiently for His plans to unfold, and that's exactly what we should do.

Sometimes, patience is the price we pay for being responsible adults, and that's as it should be. After all, think how patient our heavenly Father has been with us. So the next time you find yourself drumming your fingers as you wait for a quick resolution to the challenges of everyday living, take a deep breath and ask God for patience. Be still before your Heavenly Father and trust His timetable: it's the peaceful way to live.

If you want to hear God's voice clearly and you are uncertain, then remain in His presence until He changes that uncertainty. Often much can happen during this waiting for the Lord. Sometimes He changes pride into humility; doubt into faith and peace . . . .

Corrie ten Boom

PRIORITIES FOR MY LIFE

What's good for you is good for them, too: If you want others to be patient with you, then you should treat them in the same way.

TIMELESS WISDOM FOR GODLY LIVING

The deepest spiritual lessons are not learned by His letting us have our way in the end, but by His making us wait, bearing with us in love and patience until we are able honestly to pray what He taught His disciples to pray: Thy will be done.

Elisabeth Elliot

Those who have had to wait and work for happiness seem to enjoy it more, because they never take it for granted.

Barbara Johnson

Waiting is an essential part of spiritual discipline. It can be the ultimate test of faith.

Anne Graham Lotz

Patience and encouragement come from God. And I pray that God will help you all agree with each other the way Christ Jesus wants.
Romans 15:5 NCV

When we read of the great Biblical leaders, we see that it was not uncommon for God to ask them to wait, not just a day or two, but for years, until God was ready for them to act.

Gloria Gaither

MORE WORDS FROM GOD'S WORD

But if we look forward to something we don't have yet, we must wait patiently and confidently.

Romans 8:25 NLT

Now we exhort you, brethren, warn those who are unruly, comfort the fainthearted, uphold the weak, be patient with all.

1 Thessalonians 5:14 NKJV

God has chosen you and made you his holy people. He loves you. So always do these things: Show mercy to others, be kind, humble, gentle, and patient.

Colossians 3:12 NCV

My Priorities for Life

I take seriously the Bible's instructions to be patient.

I believe that patience is not idly waiting, but that it is an activity that means watching and waiting for God to lead me.

Even when I don't understand the circumstances that confront me, I strive to wait patiently while serving the Lord.

	Check Your Priority	
High	Med.	Low
—	—	—
—	—	—
—	—	—

nce

And the Greatest of These . . .

Though I speak with the tongues of men and of angels, but have not love,
I have become sounding brass or a clanging cymbal.

1 Corinthians 13:1 NKJV

L ove is a choice. Either you choose to behave lovingly toward others . . . or not; either you behave yourself in ways that enhance your relationships . . . or not. But make no mistake: genuine love requires effort. Simply put, if you wish to build lasting relationships, you must be willing to do your part.

Since the days of Adam and Eve, God has allowed His children to make choices for themselves, and so it is with you. As you interact with family and friends, you have choices to make . . . lots of them. If you choose wisely, you'll be rewarded; if you choose unwisely, you'll bear the consequences.

Christ's words are clear: we are to love God first, and secondly, we are to love others as we love ourselves (Matthew 22:37-40). These two commands are seldom easy, and because we are imperfect beings, we often fall short. But God's Holy Word commands us to try.

The Christian path is an exercise in love and forgiveness. If we are to walk in Christ's footsteps, we must forgive those who have done us harm, and we must accept Christ's love by sharing it freely with family, friends, neighbors, and even strangers.

God does not intend for you to experience mediocre relationships; He created you for far greater things. Building lasting relationships requires compassion, wisdom, empathy, kindness, courtesy, and forgiveness. If that sounds a lot like work, it is—which is perfectly fine with God. Why? Because He knows that you are capable of doing that work, and because He knows that the fruits of your labors will enrich the lives of your loved ones and the lives of generations yet unborn.

Only joyous love redeems.

Catherine Marshall

PRIORITIES FOR MY LIFE

Do you want love to last? Then you must understand this: Genuine love requires effort. That's why those who are lazy in love are often losers in love, too!

TIMELESS WISDOM FOR GODLY LIVING

A soul cannot live without loving. It must have something to love, for it was created to love.

Catherine of Siena

To have fallen in love hints to our hearts that all of earthly life is not hopelessly fallen. Love is the laughter of God.

Beth Moore

Our times of close, uninterrupted fellowship with him are sweet—and necessary—but so are the times when we must turn our attention toward others, when we must take the reality of his love out into the world.

Debra Evans

> *Beloved, if God so loved us,*
> *we also ought to love one another.*
> 1 John 4:11 NASB

Love is a Commandment. It is a choice, a preference. If we love God with our whole hearts, how much heart have we left? If we love with our whole mind and soul and strength, how much mind and soul and strength do we have left? We must live this life now. Death changes nothing. If we do not learn to enjoy God now, we never will.

Dorothy Day

MORE WORDS FROM GOD'S WORD

Love one another deeply, from the heart.

1 Peter 1:22 NIV

May the Lord cause you to increase and abound in love for one another, and for all people.

1 Thessalonians 3:12 NASB

I pray that you, being rooted and firmly established in love, may be able to comprehend with all the saints what is the breadth and width, height and depth, and to know the Messiah's love that surpasses knowledge, so you may be filled with all the fullness of God.

Ephesians 3:17-19 Holman CSB

My Priorities for Life

As a follower of Christ, I understand that I am commanded to love other people, and I take that commandment seriously.

Because I place a high priority on my relationships, I am willing to invest the time and energy that is required to make those relationships work.

When I have been hurt by someone, I understand the importance of forgiving that person as quickly as possible and as completely as possible.

Check Your Priority		
High	Med.	Low
—	—	—
—	—	—
—	—	—

The Power of Integrity

Till I die, I will not deny my integrity.
I will maintain my righteousness and never let go of it;
my conscience will not reproach me as long as I live.

Job 27:5-6 NIV

Wise women understand that integrity is a crucial building block in the foundation of a well-lived life. Integrity is built slowly over a lifetime. It is the sum of every right decision, every honest word, every noble thought, and every heartfelt prayer. It is forged on the anvil of honorable work and polished by the twin virtues of generosity and humility. Integrity is a precious thing—difficult to build, but easy to tear down; godly women value it and protect it at all costs.

As believers in Christ, we must seek to live each day with discipline, honesty, and faith. When we do, at least two things happen: integrity becomes a habit, and God blesses us because of our obedience to Him.

Living a life of integrity isn't always the easiest way, but it is always the right way. And God clearly intends that it should be our way, too.

God never called us to naïveté. He called us to integrity . . . .
The Biblical concept of integrity emphasizes
mature innocence not childlike ignorance.

Beth Moore

In everything set them an example by doing what is good.
In your teaching show integrity, seriousness and soundness of speech
that cannot be condemned, so that those who oppose
you may be ashamed because they have nothing
bad to say about us.

Titus 2:7 NIV

PRIORITIES FOR MY LIFE

Are you ever tempted to "sugarcoat" the truth? If so, remember that God doesn't command you to be honest when it's convenient or easy to be truthful. God's Word teaches you to be honest all the time. So the next time you're tempted to bend the truth—or tempted to break it—stop yourself before you make a big mistake.

TIMELESS WISDOM FOR GODLY LIVING

The single most important element in any human relationship is honesty—with oneself, with God, and with others.

Catherine Marshall

One thing that is important for stable emotional health is honesty—with self and with others.

Joyce Meyer

We must learn, then, to relate transparently and genuinely to others because that is God's style of relating to us.

Rebecca Manley Pippert

Character cannot be developed in ease and quiet. Only through experience of trial and suffering can the soul be strengthened, vision cleared, ambition inspired, and success achieved.

Helen Keller

People with integrity have firm footing,
but those who follow crooked paths will slip and fall.
Proverbs 10:9 NLT

Our life pursuits will reflect our character and personal integrity.

Franklin Graham

MORE WORDS FROM GOD'S WORD

The integrity of the upright will guide them.

Proverbs 11:3 NKJV

Love and truth form a good leader; sound leadership is founded on loving integrity.

Proverbs 20:28 MSG

Not only so, but we also rejoice in our sufferings, because we know that suffering produces perseverance; perseverance, character; and character, hope.

Romans 5:3-4 NIV

May integrity and uprightness protect me, because my hope is in you.

Psalm 25:21 NIV

My Priorities for Life

I value the importance of being truthful with other people and with myself.

I will trust my conscience and follow it.

I will resist the temptation to follow the crowd, choosing instead to follow Jesus.

Check Your Priority		
High	Med.	Low
—	—	—
—	—	—
—	—	—

God Can Handle It

Now the God of all grace, who called you
to His eternal glory in Christ Jesus, will personally restore,
establish, strengthen, and support you.

1 Peter 5:10 Holman CSB

O f this you can be certain: God is sufficient to meet your needs. Period.

Do the demands of life seem overwhelming at times? If so, you must learn to rely not only upon your own resources but also upon the promises of your Father in heaven. God will hold your hand and walk with you and your family if you let Him. So even if your circumstances are difficult, trust the Father.

The Psalmist writes, "Weeping may endure for a night, but joy comes in the morning" (Psalm 30:5 NKJV). But when we are suffering, the morning may seem very far away. It is not. God promises that He is "near to those who have a broken heart" (Psalm 34:18 NKJV). When we are troubled, we must turn to Him, and we must encourage our friends and family members to do likewise.

If you are discouraged by the inevitable demands of life-here-on-earth, be mindful of this fact: the loving heart of God is sufficient to meet any challenge . . . including yours.

Only believe, don't fear. Our Master, Jesus,
always watches over us, and no matter what the persecution,
Jesus will surely overcome it.

Lottie Moon

*Therefore whoever hears these sayings of Mine, and does them,
I will liken him to a wise man who built his house on the rock:
and the rain descended, the floods came, and the winds blew
and beat on that house; and it did not fall,
for it was founded on the rock.*

Matthew 7:24-25 NKJV

PRIORITIES FOR MY LIFE

God can handle it. Corrie ten Boom advised, "God's all-sufficiency is a major. Your inability is a minor. Major in majors, not in minors." Enough said.

TIMELESS WISDOM FOR GODLY LIVING

When we reach the end of our strength, wisdom, and personal resources, we enter into the beginning of his glorious provisions.

Patsy Clairmont

God will take care of everything—the rest is up to you.

Lisa Whelchel

It is enough to know his promise that he will give what is good—he knows so much more about that than we do.

Elisabeth Elliot

But God wants you to realize that he is tending to your needs—not just when your helplessness is thick and tangible—but even in those times when you feel the most in control.

Cheri Fuller

The LORD is my strength and song, and He has become my salvation; He is my God, and I will praise Him . . .
Exodus 15:2 NKJV

When you live a surrendered life, God is willing and able to provide for your every need.

Corrie ten Boom

MORE WORDS FROM GOD'S WORD

Peace, peace to you, and peace to your helpers! For your God helps you.

1 Chronicles 12:18 NKJV

He gives power to the weak, and to those who have no might He increases strength.

Isaiah 40:29 NKJV

I am able to do all things through Him who strengthens me.

Philippians 4:13 Holman CSB

The Lord is my rock, my fortress and my Savior; my God is my rock in whom I find protection. He is my shield, the strength of my salvation, and my stronghold.

Psalm 18:2 NLT

My Priorities for Life

I expect God to be sufficient for all my needs.

When I place my faith in an all-sufficient God, life becomes a grand adventure.

Worship reminds me of the awesome support of God. I worship Him daily, and seek to allow Him to work through me.

Check Your Priority		
High	Med.	Low
—	—	—
—	—	—
—	—	—

A Heart Filled with Joy

Let the hearts of those who seek the Lord rejoice.
Look to the Lord and his strength; seek his face always.

1 Chronicles 16:10-11 NIV

Christ made it clear to His followers: He intended that His joy would become their joy. And it still holds true today: Christ intends that His believers share His love with His joy in their hearts. Yet sometimes, amid the inevitable hustle and bustle of daily life, we can forfeit—albeit temporarily—the joy of Christ as we wrestle with the challenges of daily living.

Happiness depends less upon our circumstances than upon our thoughts. When we turn our thoughts to God, to His gifts, and to His glorious creation, we experience the joy that God intends for His children. But, when we focus on the negative aspects of life, we suffer needlessly.

Psalm 100 reminds us that, as believers, we have every reason to celebrate: "Shout for joy to the LORD, all the earth. Worship the LORD with gladness" (v. 1-2 NIV). And C. H. Spurgeon, the renowned 19th century English clergymen, advised, "The Lord is glad to open the gate to every knocking soul. It opens very freely; its hinges are not rusted; no bolts secure it. Have faith and enter at this moment through holy courage. If you knock with a heavy heart, you shall yet sing with joy of spirit. Never be discouraged!"

So today, if your heart is heavy, open the door of your soul to Christ. He will give you peace and joy. And, if you already have the joy of Christ in your heart, share it freely, just as Christ freely shared His joy with you.

It is the definition of joy to be able to offer back to God
the essence of what he's placed in you, be that creativity
or a love of ideas or a compassionate heart
or the gift of hospitality.

Paula Rinehart

PRIORITIES FOR MY LIFE

Joy begins with a choice: the choice to establish a genuine relationship with God and His Son. As Amy Carmichael correctly observed, "Joy is not gush; joy is not mere jolliness. Joy is perfect acquiescence, acceptance, and rest in God's will, whatever comes."

ΛELESS WISDOM FOR GODLY LIVING

For what we dare to give to one another in love enriches us at the time, stays behind to comfort and help at our parting, yet still goes on to heaven—a seed to flower in eternity, bringing perennial joy.

Susan Lenzkes

The Christian lifestyle is not one of legalistic do's and don'ts, but one that is positive, attractive, and joyful.

Vonette Bright

Finding joy means first of all finding Jesus.

Jill Briscoe

Joy is the characteristic by which God uses us to re-make the distressing into the desired, the discarded into the creative. Joy is prayer—joy is strength—joy is love—joy is a net of love by which you can catch souls.

Mother Teresa

> *Rejoice, and be exceeding glad:*
> *for great is your reward in heaven . . . .*
> Matthew 5:12 KJV

The greatest honor you can give Almighty God is to live gladly and joyfully because of the knowledge of His love.

Juliana of Norwich

MORE WORDS FROM GOD'S WORD

Rejoice evermore. Pray without ceasing. In every thing give thanks: for this is the will of God in Christ Jesus concerning you.

1 Thessalonians 5:16-18 KJV

These things I have spoken to you, that My joy may remain in you, and that your joy may be full.

John 15:11 NKJV

Always be full of joy in the Lord. I say it again—rejoice!

Philippians 4:4 NLT

Shout for joy to the LORD, all the earth. Worship the LORD with gladness; come before him with joyful songs.

Psalm 100:1-2 NIV

My Priorities for Life

Because I am a Christian, I believe that my joy does not depend upon my circumstances, but on my relationship with God.

When I count my blessings and thank God for those blessings, I am more joyful.

When I participate in regular heartfelt worship, I am more joyful.

Check Your Priority		
High	Med.	Low
—	—	—
—	—	—
—	—	—

Family Ties

He who brings trouble on his family will inherit only wind . . . .

Proverbs 11:29 NIV

As every woman knows, home life is a mixture of conversations, mediations, irritations, deliberations, commiserations, frustrations, negotiations and celebrations. In other words, the life of the typical woman is incredibly varied.

Certainly, in the life of every family, there are moments of frustration and disappointment. Lots of them. But, for those who are lucky enough to live in the presence of a close-knit, caring clan, the rewards far outweigh the frustrations. That's why we pray fervently for our family members, and that's why we love them despite their faults.

Even on those difficult days when your to-do list is full and your nerves are frayed, you must never forget this fact: your clan is God's gift to you. That little band of men, women, kids, and babies is a priceless treasure on temporary loan from the Father above. Give thanks to the Giver for the gift of family...and act _ngly.

Living life with a consistent spiritual walk
deeply influences those we love most.

Vonette Bright

When God asks someone to do something for Him
entailing sacrifice, He makes up for it in surprising ways.
Though He has led Bill all over the world to preach the gospel,
He has not forgotten the little family in the mountains
of North Carolina.

Ruth Bell Graham

PRIORITIES FOR MY LIFE

Today, think about the importance of saying "yes" to your family
even if it means saying "no" to other obligations.

TIMELESS WISDOM FOR GODLY LIVING

There is so much compassion and understanding that is gained when we've experienced God's grace firsthand within our own families.

Lisa Whelchel

One way or the other, God, who thought up the family in the first place, has the very best idea of how to bring sense to the chaos of broken relationships we see all around us. I really believe that if I remain still and listen a lot, He will share some solutions with me so I can share them with others.

Jill Briscoe

The only true source of meaning in life is found in love for God and His son Jesus Christ, and love for mankind, beginning with our own families.

James Dobson

. . . these should learn first of all to put their religion into practice by caring for their own family . . . .
1 Timothy 5:4 NIV

For whatever life holds for you and your family in the coming days, weave the unfailing fabric of God's Word through your heart and mind. It will hold strong, even if the rest of life unravels.

Gigi Graham Tchividjian

MORE WORDS FROM GOD'S WORD

You must choose for yourselves today whom you will serve . . . as for me and my family, we will serve the Lord.

Joshua 24:15 NCV

Every kingdom divided against itself will be ruined, and every city or household divided against itself will not stand.

Matthew 12:25 NIV

Let love and faithfulness never leave you . . . write them on the tablet of your heart.

Proverbs 3:3 NIV

The one who brings ruin on his household will inherit the wind.

Proverbs 11:29 Holman CSB

My Priorities for Life

I place a high priority on spending time with my family.

I think that my family should make God its number one priority.

I look for ways to say—and to show—my family I love them.

Check Your Priority		
High	Med.	Low
—	—	—
—	—	—
—	—	—

Aiming High

Live full lives, full in the fullness of God. God can do anything,
you know—far more than you could ever imagine or guess or request
in your wildest dreams! He does it not by pushing us around but
by working within us, his Spirit deeply and gently within us.

Ephesians 3:19-20 MSG

Are you willing to entertain the possibility that God has big plans in store for you? Hopefully so. Yet sometimes, especially if you've recently experienced a life-altering disappointment, you may find it difficult to envision a brighter future for yourself and your family. If so, it's time to reconsider your own capabilities . . . and God's.

Your heavenly Father created you with unique gifts and untapped talents; your job is to tap them. When you do, you'll begin to feel an increasing sense of confidence in yourself and in your future. As the old saying goes, if you feed your faith, your doubts will starve to death.

On occasion, you will face the inevitable disappointments of life. And sometimes, you must endure life-altering personal losses that leave you breathless. On such occasions, you may be tempted to abandon your dreams. Don't do it! Instead, trust that God is preparing you for greater things.

Concentration camp survivor Corrie ten Boom observed, "Every experience God gives us, every person He brings into our lives, is the perfect preparation for the future that only He can see." These words apply to you.

Are you excited about the opportunities of today and thrilled by the possibilities of tomorrow? Do you confidently expect God to lead you to a place of abundance, peace, and joy? And, when your days on earth are over, do you expect to receive the priceless gift of eternal life? If you trust God's promises, and if you have welcomed God's Son into your heart, then you believe that your future is intensely and eternally bright.

It takes courage to dream big dreams. You will discover that courage when you do three things: accept the past, trust God to handle the future, and make the most of the time He has given you today.

Nothing is too difficult for God, and no dreams are too big for Him—not even yours. So start living—and dreaming—accordingly.

The future lies all before us. Shall it only be a slight advance upon what we usually do? Ought it not to be a bound, a leap forward to altitudes of endeavor and success undreamed of before?

Annie Armstrong

PRIORITIES FOR MY LIFE

Be a dreamer. Your attitude toward the future will help create your future. So think realistically about yourself (and your situation) but focus your thoughts on hopes, not fears. When you do, you'll put the self-fulfilling prophecy to work for you.

TIMELESS WISDOM FOR GODLY LIVING

Allow your dreams a place in your prayers and plans. God-given dreams can help you move into the future He is preparing for you.

Barbara Johnson

God created us with an overwhelming desire to soar. He designed us to be tremendously productive and "to mount up with wings like eagles," realistically dreaming of what He can do with our potential.

Carol Kent

Sometimes our dreams were so big that it took two people to dream them.

Marie T. Freeman

You pay God a compliment by asking great things of Him.

St. Teresa of Avila

I came so they can have real and eternal life, more and better life than they ever dreamed of.
John 10:10 MSG

You cannot out-dream God.

John Eldredge

MORE WORDS FROM GOD'S WORD

It is pleasant to see dreams come true, but fools will not turn from evil to attain them.

Proverbs 13:19 NLT

The Lord values those who fear Him, those who put their hope in His faithful love.

Psalm 147:11 Holman CSB

May He grant you according to your heart's desire, and fulfill all your purpose.

Psalm 20:4 NKJV

My Priorities for Life

	Check Your Priority	
High	Med.	Low

I will place my hopes and dreams in God.

— — —

I prayerfully seek to understand God's plans for my life.

— — —

I work to know God's plan for my life, and I work to fulfill that plan.

— — —

I try not to place limitations on myself, and I refuse to place limitations on God's power to use me for His purposes.

— — —

Laughter is the Best Medicine

There is a time for everything, and a season for every activity
under heaven . . . a time to weep and a time to laugh,
a time to mourn and a time to dance . . . .

Ecclesiastes 3:1,4 NIV

Laughter, as the old saying goes, is medicine for the soul. But sometimes, amid the stresses of the day, we forget to take our medicine. Instead of viewing our world with a mixture of optimism and humor, we allow worries and distractions to rob us of the joy that God intends for our lives.

If you're suffering from the inevitable demands of 21st-century life, you know all too well that a good laugh may seem hard to find. But it need not be so. And if you're having trouble getting your funny bone in gear, here's a helpful hint: LIGHTEN UP AND DON'T TAKE THINGS SO SERIOUSLY (especially yourself). When you do, you'll soon learn that everything goes better when you learn to laugh at yourself and when you learn to find humor in life's little mishaps.

Your life is either a comedy or a tragedy, depending upon how you look at it. Make yours a comedy. So today, as a gift to ʸourself, to your spouse, and to your kids, approach life with a smile on your lips and a chuckle in your heart. After all, God created laughter for a very good reason . . . and since the Father knows best, you might as well laugh while you can.

He who laughs lasts—he who doesn't, doesn't.

Marie T. Freeman

Shout for joy to the LORD, all the earth, burst into jubilant song with music; make music to the LORD with the harp, with the harp and the sound of singing, with trumpets and the blast of the ram's horn—shout for joy before the LORD, the King.

Psalm 98:4-6 NIV

PRIORITIES FOR MY LIFE

Learn to laugh at life. Life has a lighter side—look for it, especially when times are tough. Laughter is medicine for the soul, so take your medicine early and often.

TIMELESS WISDOM FOR GODLY LIVING

I think everybody ought to be a laughing Christian. I'm convinced that there's just one place where there's not any laughter, and that's hell.

Jerry Clower

Laughter is the language of the young at heart and the antidote to what ails us.

Barbara Johnson

I want to encourage you in these days with your family to lighten up and enjoy. Laugh a little bit; it might just set you free.

Dennis Swanberg

You don't have to be happy to laugh. You become happy because you laugh.

Barbara Johnson

A happy heart is like good medicine.
Proverbs 17:22 NCV

Laughter is like internal jogging—in many ways as good as physical exercise.

Joyce Meyer

MORE WORDS FROM GOD'S WORD

Shout for joy to the LORD, all the earth, burst into jubilant song with music; make music to the LORD with the harp, with the harp and the sound of singing, with trumpets and the blast of the ram's horn—shout for joy before the LORD, the King.

Psalm 98:4-6 NIV

Nehemiah said, "Go and enjoy choice food and sweet drinks, and send some to those who have nothing prepared. This day is sacred to our Lord. Do not grieve, for the joy of the LORD is your strength."

Nehemiah 8:10 NIV

Clap your hands, all you nations; shout to God with cries of joy.

Psalm 47:1 NIV

My Priorities for Life

I understand the importance of looking for the humor in most situations.

I will think about ways that I can use humor as a way to improve my own life and the lives of the people around me.

I look for the joy and humor in everyday life.

Check Your Priority		
High	Med.	Low
—	—	—
—	—	—
—	—	—

When Doubts Creep In

When doubts filled my mind,
your comfort gave me renewed hope and cheer.

Psalm 94:19 NLT

Have you ever wondered if God hears your prayers? If so, you're not the first person to have questions like that. Doubts come in several shapes and sizes: doubts about God, doubts about the future, and doubts about your own abilities, for starters. And what, precisely, does God's Word say in response to these doubts? The Bible is clear: when you are beset by doubts, of whatever kind, you must draw yourself nearer to God through worship and through prayer. When you do, God, the loving Father who has never left your side, draws ever closer to you (James 4:8).

Is prayer an integral part of your daily life or is it a hit-or-miss habit? Do you "pray without ceasing," or is prayer an afterthought? If your prayer life leaves something to be desired, you're robbing yourself of a deeper relationship with God. And how can you rectify that situation? By praying more frequently and more fervently.

The quality of your spiritual life will be in direct proportion to the quality of your prayer life: the more you pray, the closer you will feel to God. So today, instead of turning things over in your mind, turn them over to God in prayer. Instead of worrying about your next decision, ask God to lead the way. Don't limit your prayers to the dinner table or the bedside table. Pray constantly about things great and small. When you do, your Heavenly Father will take care of you . . . and your doubts will take care of themselves.

Unconfessed sin in your life will cause you to doubt.

Anne Graham Lotz

Come! He said. And climbing out of the boat, Peter started walking on the water and came toward Jesus. But when he saw the strength of the wind, he was afraid. And beginning to sink he cried out, "Lord, save me!" Immediately Jesus reached out His hand, caught hold of him, and said to him, "You of little faith, why did you doubt?" When they got into the boat, the wind ceased.

Matthew 14:29-32 Holman CSB

PRIORITIES FOR MY LIFE

Are you sincerely looking for a way to address your doubts? Try Bible Study, prayer, and worship.

TIMELESS WISDOM FOR GODLY LIVING

Just as I am, though tossed about with many a conflict, many a doubt, fightings and fears within, without, O Lamb of God, I come, I come.

Charlotte Elliott

I was learning something important: we are most vulnerable to the piercing winds of doubt when we distance ourselves from the mission and fellowship to which Christ has called us. Our night of discouragement will seem endless and our task impossible, unless we recognize that He stands in our midst.

Joni Eareckson Tada

We must lay our questions, frustrations, anxieties, and impotence at the feet of God and wait for His answer. And then receiving it, we must live by faith.

Kay Arthur

Purify your hearts, ye double-minded.
James 4:8 KJV

There is a difference between doubt and unbelief. Doubt is a matter of mind: we cannot understand what God is doing or why He is doing it. Unbelief is a matter of will: we refuse to believe God's Word and obey what He tells us to do.

Warren Wiersbe

MORE WORDS FROM GOD'S WORD

If you don't know what you're doing, pray to the Father. He loves to help. You'll get his help, and won't be condescended to when you ask for it. Ask boldly, believingly, without a second thought. People who "worry their prayers" are like wind-whipped waves. Don't think you're going to get anything from the Master that way, adrift at sea, keeping all your options open.

James 1:5-8 MSG

Jesus said, "Because you have seen Me, you have believed. Blessed are those who believe without seeing."

John 20:29 Holman CSB

My Priorities for Life

When I have doubts, I believe that it is important to take those doubts to the Lord.

Even when I cannot understand why certain things happen, I trust God's plan for my life and the world.

I understand the importance of focusing my thoughts and prayers on the opportunities that God has placed before me.

Check Your Priority		
High	Med.	Low
—	—	—
—	—	—
—	—	—

God's Surprising Plans

And we know that in all things God works for the good of those who love him, who have been called according to his purpose.

Romans 8:28 NIV

D o you want to experience a life filled with abundance and peace? If so, here's a word of warning: you'll need to resist the temptation to do things "your way" and commit, instead, to do things God's way.

God has plans for your life. Big plans. But He won't force you to follow His will; to the contrary, He has given you free will, the ability to make decisions on your own. With the freedom to choose comes the responsibility of living with the consequences of the choices you make.

The most important decision of your life is, of course, your commitment to accept Jesus Christ as your personal Lord and Savior. And once your eternal destiny is secured, you will undoubtedly ask yourself the question "What now, Lord?" If you earnestly seek God's will for your life, you will find it . . . in time.

When you make the decision to seek God's will for your life, you will contemplate His Word, and you will be watchful for His signs. You will associate with fellow believers who will encourage your spiritual growth. And, you will listen to that inner voice that speaks to you in the quiet moments of your daily devotionals.

Sometimes, God's plans are crystal clear, but other times, He leads you through the wilderness before He delivers you to the Promised Land. So be patient, keep searching, and keep praying. If you do, then in time, God will answer your prayers and make His plans known.

God is right here, and He intends to use you in wonderful, unexpected ways. You'll discover those plans by doing things His way . . . and you'll be eternally grateful that you did.

If we stay with the Lord, enduring to the end of
His great plan for us, we will enjoy the rest that
results from living in the kingdom of God.

Serita Ann Jakes

PRIORITIES FOR MY LIFE

Waiting faithfully for God's plan to unfold is more important than understanding God's plan. Ruth Bell Graham once said, "When I am dealing with an all-powerful, all-knowing God, I, as a mere mortal, must offer my petitions not only with persistence, but also with patience. Someday I'll know why." Even when you can't understand God's plans, you must trust Him and never lose faith!

TIMELESS WISDOM FOR GODLY LIVING

The secret you stumble on is this: If, once hurt, you open your heart and let God take you by the hand, he will lead you to a better place than you have known.

Paula Rinehart

There is something incredibly comforting about knowing that the Creator is in control of your life.

Lisa Whelchel

God specializes in things fresh and firsthand. His plans for you this year may outshine those of the past. He's prepared to fill your days with reasons to give Him praise.

Joni Eareckson Tada

Teach me Your way, O Lord; I will walk in Your truth.
Psalm 86:11 NKJV

I'm convinced that there is nothing that can happen to me in this life that is not precisely designed by a sovereign Lord to give me the opportunity to learn to know Him.

Elisabeth Elliot

MORE WORDS FROM GOD'S WORD

The Lord shatters the plans of nations and thwarts all their schemes. But the Lord's plans stand firm forever; his intentions can never be shaken.

Psalm 33:10-11 NLT

Trust the Lord your God with all your heart and lean not on your own understanding; in all your ways acknowledge him, and he will make your paths straight.

Proverbs 3:5-6 NIV

There is one thing I always do. Forgetting the past and straining toward what is ahead, I keep trying to reach the goal and get the prize for which God called me . . . .

Philippians 3:13–14 NCV

My Priorities for Life

Since I trust that God's plans have eternal ramifications, I will seek His will for my life.

Since I believe that God has a plan for my day, I set aside quiet time each morning in order to seek His will for my life.

My plans are imperfect; God's plans are perfect; so I choose to trust God.

Check Your Priority		
High	Med.	Low
—	—	—
—	—	—
—	—	—

Asking and Accepting

If you need wisdom—if you want to know what
God wants you to do—ask him, and he will gladly tell you.
He will not resent your asking.

James 1:5 NLT

J esus made it clear to His disciples: they should petition God to meet their needs. So should we. Genuine, heartfelt prayer produces powerful changes in us and in our world. When we lift our hearts to God, we open ourselves to a never-ending source of divine wisdom and infinite love.

God can do great things through you if you have the courage to ask Him (and the determination to keep asking Him). But don't expect Him to do all the work. When you do your part, He will do His part. And when He does, expect a miracle.

How often do you ask God for His help and His wisdom? Occasionally? Intermittently? Whenever you experience a crisis? Hopefully not. Hopefully, you've acquired the habit of asking for God's assistance early and often. And hopefully, you have learned to seek His guidance in every aspect of your life.

The Bible promises that God will guide you if you let Him. Your job is to let Him. But sometimes, you will be tempted to do otherwise. Sometimes, you'll be tempted to go along with the crowd; other times, you'll be tempted to do things your way, not God's way. When you feel those temptations, resist them.

God stands at the door and waits. When you knock, He opens. When you ask, He answers. Your task, of course, is to seek His guidance prayerfully, confidently, and often.

God uses our most stumbling, faltering faith-steps as the open door to His doing for us "more than we ask or think."

Catherine Marshall

You fathers—if your children ask for a fish, do you give them a snake instead? Or if they ask for an egg, do you give them a scorpion? Of course not! If you sinful people know how to give good gifts to your children, how much more will your heavenly Father give the Holy Spirit to those who ask him.

Luke 11:11-13 NLT

PRIORITIES FOR MY LIFE

If you want more from life, ask more from God. If you're seeking a worthy goal, ask for God's help—and keep asking—until He answers your prayers.

TIMELESS WISDOM FOR GODLY LIVING

When will we realize that we're not troubling God with our questions and concerns? His heart is open to hear us—his touch nearer than our next thought—as if no one in the world existed but us. Our very personal God wants to hear from us personally.

Gigi Graham Tchividjian

When trials come your way—as inevitably they will—do not run away. Run to your God and Father.

Kay Arthur

When you ask God to do something, don't ask timidly; put your whole heart into it.

Marie T. Freeman

From now on, whatever you request along the lines of who I am and what I am doing, I'll do it. That's how the Father will be seen for who he is in the Son. I mean it. Whatever you request in this way, I'll do.

John 14:13-14 MSG

By asking in Jesus' name, we're making a request not only in His authority, but also for His interests and His benefit.

Shirley Dobson

MORE WORDS FROM GOD'S WORD

You did not choose me, but I chose you and appointed you to go and bear fruit—fruit that will last. Then the Father will give you whatever you ask in my name.

John 15:16 NIV

Until now you have not asked for anything in my name. Ask and you will receive, so that your joy will be the fullest possible joy.

John 16:24 NCV

Do not worry about anything, but pray and ask God for everything you need, always giving thanks.

Philippians 4:6 NCV

You do not have, because you do not ask God.

James 4:2 NIV

My Priorities for Life

I am willing to petition God about matters large and small.

When I ask God for help, I also understand that His will must be done.

I will consistently call upon God for His help.

Check Your Priority		
High	Med.	Low
—	—	—
—	—	—
—	—	—

This Is the Day

This is the day the LORD has made; let us rejoice and be glad in it.

Psalm 118:24 NIV

The familiar words of Psalm 118:24 remind us of a profound yet simple truth: God created this day, and it's up to each of us to rejoice and to be grateful.

For Christian believers, every day begins and ends with God and His Son. Christ came to this earth to give us abundant life and eternal salvation. We give thanks to our Maker when we treasure each day and use it to the fullest.

This day is a gift from God. How will you use it? Will you celebrate God's gifts and obey His commandments? Will you share words of encouragement and hope with all who cross your path? Will you share the Good News of the risen Christ? Will you trust in the Father and praise His glorious handiwork? The answer to these questions will determine, to a surprising extent, the direction and the quality of your day.

So whatever this day holds for you, begin it and end it with God as your partner and Christ as your Savior. And throughout the day, give thanks to the One who created you and saved you. God's love for you is infinite. Accept it joyously and be thankful.

May your day be fashioned with joy, sprinkled with dreams,
and touched by the miracle of love.

Barbara Johnson

Commitment to His lordship on Easter, at revivals,
or even every Sunday is not enough. We must choose this day—
and every day—whom we will serve. This deliberate act of
the will is the inevitable choice between
habitual fellowship and habitual failure.

Beth Moore

PRIORITIES FOR MY LIFE

Take time to celebrate another day of life. And while you're at it,
encourage your family and friends to join in the celebration.

TIMELESS WISDOM FOR GODLY LIVING

Every day we live is a priceless gift of God, loaded with possibilities to learn something new, to gain fresh insights.

Dale Evans Rogers

Today is mine. Tomorrow is none of my business. If I peer anxiously into the fog of the future, I will strain my spiritual eyes so that I will not see clearly what is required of me now.

Elisabeth Elliot

Each day, each moment is so pregnant with eternity that if we "tune in" to it, we can hardly contain the joy.

Gloria Gaither

While it is daytime, we must continue doing the work of the One who sent me. Night is coming, when no one can work.

John 9:4 NCV

Live today fully, expressing gratitude for all you have been, all you are right now, and all you are becoming.

Melodie Beattie

MORE WORDS FROM GOD'S WORD

So don't worry about tomorrow, for tomorrow will bring its own worries. Today's trouble is enough for today.

Matthew 6:34 NLT

You will show me the way of life, granting me the joy of your presence and the pleasures of living with you forever.

Psalm 16:11 NLT

Encourage one another daily, as long as it is Today . . . .

Hebrews 3:13 NIV

My Priorities for Life

I will consider this day—and every day—to be another opportunity to celebrate life.

I will treat this day as a priceless gift . . . and I will use my time accordingly.

I will take time each day to thank God for the opportunity to live joyfully and abundantly.

I will encourage my family and friends to join in today's celebration of life.

Check Your Priority		
High	Med.	Low
—	—	—
—	—	—
—	—	—
—	—	—

Making Worship a High Priority

Worship the Lord your God and . . . serve Him only.

Matthew 4:10 Holman CSB

All of humanity is engaged in worship. The question is not whether we worship, but what we worship. Wise men and women choose to worship God. When they do, they are blessed with a plentiful harvest of joy, peace, and abundance. Other people choose to distance themselves from God by foolishly worshiping things that are intended to bring personal gratification but not spiritual gratification. Such choices often have tragic consequences.

If we place our love for material possessions above our love for God—or if we yield to the countless temptations of this world—we find ourselves engaged in a struggle between good and evil, a clash between God and Satan. Our responses to these struggles have implications that echo throughout our families and throughout our communities.

How can we ensure that we cast our lot with God? We do so, in part, by the practice of regular, purposeful worship in the company of fellow believers. When we worship God faithfully and fervently, we are blessed. When we fail to worship God, for whatever reason, we forfeit the spiritual gifts that He intends for us.

We must worship our heavenly Father, not just with our words, but also with deeds. We must honor Him, praise Him, and obey Him. As we seek to find purpose and meaning for our lives, we must first seek His purpose and His will. For believers, God comes first. Always first.

Do you place a high value on the practice of worship? Hopefully so. After all, every day provides countless opportunities to put God where He belongs: at the very center of your life. It's up to you to worship God seven days a week; anything less is simply not enough.

It's our privilege to not only raise our hands in worship but also to combine the visible with the invisible in a rising stream of praise and adoration sent directly to our Father.

Shirley Dobson

PRIORITIES FOR MY LIFE

Worship is not meant to be boxed up in a church building on Sunday morning. To the contrary, praise and worship should be woven into the very fabric of your day. Do you take time each day to worship your Father in heaven, or do you wait until Sunday morning to praise Him for His blessings? The answer to this question will, in large part, determine the quality and direction of your life. So worship accordingly.

TIMELESS WISDOM FOR GODLY LIVING

Worship is about rekindling an ashen heart into a blazing fire.

Liz Curtis Higgs

Worship always empowers the worshiper with a greater revelation of the object of her desire.

Lisa Bevere

In the sanctuary, we discover beauty: the beauty of His presence.

Kay Arthur

God asks that we worship Him with our concentrated minds as well as with our wills and emotions. A divided and scattered mind is not effective.

Catherine Marshall

God lifted him high and honored him far beyond anyone or anything, ever, so that all created beings in heaven and earth, even those long ago dead and buried, will bow in worship before this Jesus Christ, and call out in praise that he is the Master of all, to the glorious honor of God the Father.

Philippians 2:9-11 MSG

Worship is God-centered, aware of one another only in that deep, joyous awareness of being caught up together in God.

Anne Ortlund

MORE WORDS FROM GOD'S WORD

Worship the Lord with gladness. Come before him, singing with joy. Acknowledge that the Lord is God! He made us, and we are his. We are his people, the sheep of his pasture.

Psalm 100:2-3 NLT

A time is coming and has now come when the true worshipers will worship the Father in spirit and truth, for they are the kind of worshipers the Father seeks. God is spirit, and his worshipers must worship in spirit and in truth.

John 4:23-24 NIV

Blessed are they which do hunger and thirst after righteousness: for they shall be filled.

Matthew 5:6 KJV

My Priorities for Life

I believe that it is important to worship God every day of the week, not just on Sundays.

I feel that it is important to worship regularly with the community of believers.

I have a quiet place where I can go, a place where God seems especially close.

Check Your Priority		
High	Med.	Low
—	—	—
—	—	—
—	—	—

The Power of Simplicity

You've gotten a reputation as a bad-news people, you people of Judah and Israel, but I'm coming to save you. From now on, you're the good-news people. Don't be afraid. Keep a firm grip on what I'm doing." Keep Your Lives Simple and Honest.

Zechariah 8:13 MSG

You live in a world where simplicity is in short supply. Think for a moment about the complexity of your life and compare it to the lives of your ancestors. Certainly, you are the beneficiary of many technological innovations, but these innovations have a price: in all likelihood, your world is highly complex. Consider the following:

1. From the moment you wake up in the morning until the time you lay your head on the pillow at night, you are the target of an endless stream of advertising information. Each message is intended to grab your attention in order to convince you to purchase things you didn't know you needed (and probably don't!) 2. Essential aspects of your life, including personal matters such as health care, are subject to an ever-increasing flood of rules and regulations. 3. Unless you take firm control of your time and your life, you may be overwhelmed by a tidal wave of complexity that threatens your happiness.

Is yours a life of moderation or accumulation? Are you more interested in the possessions you can acquire or in the person you can become? The answers to these questions will determine the direction of your day and, in time, the direction of your life.

If your material possessions are somehow distancing you from God, discard them. If your outside interests leave you too little time for your family or your Creator, slow down the merry-go-round, or better yet, get off the merry-go-round completely. Remember: God wants your full attention, and He wants it today, so don't let anybody or anything get in His way.

I am beginning to learn that it is the sweet, simple things of life which are the real ones after all.

Laura Ingalls Wilder

PRIORITIES FOR MY LIFE

Simplicity and peace . . . these two concepts are closely related; complexity and peace are not.

TIMELESS WISDOM FOR GODLY LIVING

Clarity is power.

Laurie Beth Jones

Nobody is going to simplify your life for you. You've got to simplify things for yourself.

Marie T. Freeman

Some of my greatest spiritual moments have been inspired by the unexpected and the simple.

Marilyn Meberg

God may be in the process of pruning something out of your life at this very moment. If this is the case, don't fight it. Instead, welcome it, for His pruning will make you more fruitful and bring greater glory to the Father.

Rick Yohn

> *A simple life in the Fear-of-God is better than a rich life with a ton of headaches.*
> Proverbs 15:16 MSG

Perhaps too much of everything is as bad as too little.

Edna Ferber

MORE WORDS FROM GOD'S WORD

But he's already made it plain how to live, what to do, what God is looking for in men and women. It's quite simple: Do what is fair and just to your neighbor, be compassionate and loyal in your love, and don't take yourself too seriously—take God seriously.

Micah 6:8 MSG

We brought nothing into the world, so we can take nothing out. But, if we have food and clothes, we will be satisfied with that.

1 Timothy 6:7-8 NCV

Then Jesus said to them, "Be careful and guard against all kinds of greed. Life is not measured by how much one owns."

Luke 12:15 NCV

My Priorities for Life

	Check Your Priority	
High	Med.	Low

I value the benefits of simplicity.

— — —

I understand that the world leads me toward a life of complexity and stress, but I also know that God leads me toward simplicity and peace.

— — —

I understand that the accumulation of material possessions does not ensure a joyful life; it is my relationship with God (and my obedience to Him) that brings me abundance and joy.

— — —

Healthy Relationships

How wonderful, how beautiful, when brothers and sisters get along!

Psalm 133:1 MSG

Emotional health is contagious, and so is emotional distress. If you're fortunate enough to be surrounded by family members and friends who celebrate life and praise God, consider yourself profoundly blessed. But, if you find yourself caught in an unhealthy relationship, it's time to look realistically at your situation and begin making changes.

Don't worry about changing other people: you can't do it. What you can do is conduct yourself in a responsible fashion and insist that other people treat you with the dignity and consideration that you deserve.

In a perfect world filled with perfect people, our relationships, too, would be perfect. But none of us are perfect and neither are our relationships . . . and that's okay. As we work to make our imperfect relationships a little happier and healthier, we grow as individuals and as families. But, if we find ourselves in relationships that are debilitating or dangerous, then changes must be made, and soon.

If you find yourself caught up in a personal relationship that is bringing havoc into your life, and if you can't seem to find the courage to do something about it, don't hesitate to consult your pastor. Or, you may seek the advice of a trusted friend or a professionally trained counselor. But whatever you do, don't be satisfied with the status quo.

God has grand plans for your life; He has promised you the joy and abundance that can be yours through Him. But to fully experience God's gifts, you need happy, emotionally healthy people to share them with. It's up to you to make sure that you do your part to build the kinds of relationships that will bring abundance to you, to your family, and to God's world.

Cherish your human connections:
your relationships with friends and family.

Barbara Bush

PRIORITIES FOR MY LIFE

Never accept blatant dishonesty as a part of any relationship, and never accept physical or emotional abuse from anyone, especially those people who are closest to you.

TIMELESS WISDOM FOR GODLY LIVING

Always stay connected to people and seek out things that bring you joy. Dream with abandon. Pray confidently.

Barbara Johnson

The single most important element in any human relationship is honesty—with oneself, with God, and with others.

Catherine Marshall

The love life of the Christian is a crucial battleground. There, if nowhere else, it will be determined who is Lord: the world, the self, and the devil—or the Lord Christ.

Elisabeth Elliot

Line by line, moment by moment, special times are etched into our memories in the permanent ink of everlasting love in our relationships.

Gloria Gaither

Love does no harm to its neighbor.
Therefore love is the fulfillment of the law.
Romans 13:10 NIV

It is my calling to treat every human being with grace and dignity, to treat every person, whether encountered in a palace or a gas station, as a life made in the image of God.

Sheila Walsh

MORE WORDS FROM GOD'S WORD

Do not be unequally yoked together with unbelievers. For what fellowship has righteousness with lawlessness? And what communion has light with darkness?

2 Corinthians 6:14 NKJV

Regarding life together and getting along with each other, you don't need me to tell you what to do. You're God-taught in these matters. Just love one another!

1 Thessalonians 4:9 MSG

Carry each other's burdens, and in this way you will fulfill the law of Christ.

Galatians 6:2 NIV

My Priorities for Life

I believe that it takes time and effort to build strong relationships.

I believe effective communication is the cornerstone of good relationships.

I believe some relationships bring chaos into my life, and I believe that these types of relationships should be avoided if possible.

Check Your Priority		
High	Med.	Low
—	—	—
—	—	—
—	—	—

Following in His Footsteps

Be imitators of God, therefore, as dearly loved children.

Ephesians 5:1 NIV

When Jesus addressed His disciples, He warned that each one must, "take up his cross and follow me." The disciples must have known exactly what the Master meant. In Jesus' day, prisoners were forced to carry their own crosses to the location where they would be put to death. Thus, Christ's message was clear: in order to follow Him, Christ's disciples must deny themselves and, instead, trust Him completely. Nothing has changed since then.

If we are to be disciples of Christ, we must trust Him and place Him at very center of our beings. Jesus never comes "next." He is always first. The paradox, of course, is that only by sacrificing ourselves to Him do we gain salvation for ourselves.

The 19th-century writer Hannah Whitall Smith observed, "The crucial question for each of us is this: What do you think of Jesus, and do you yet have a personal acquaintance with Him?" Indeed, the answer to that question will determine the quality, the course, and the direction of your life today and for all eternity.

Jesus has called upon believers of every generation (and that includes you) to walk with Him. Jesus promises that when you follow in His footsteps, He will teach you how to live freely and lightly (Matthew 11:28-30). And when Jesus makes a promise, you can depend upon it.

Are you worried or anxious? Be confident in the power of Christ. He will never desert you. Are you discouraged? Be courageous and call upon your Savior. He will protect you and use you according to His purposes. Do you seek to be a worthy disciple of the One from Galilee? Then pick up His cross today and every day of your life. When you do, He will bless you now . . . and forever.

Jesus challenges you and me to keep our focus
daily on the cross of His will if we want to be His disciples.

Anne Graham Lotz

PRIORITIES FOR MY LIFE

If you want to be a disciple of Christ . . . follow in His footsteps, obey His commandments, and share His never-ending love.

TIMELESS WISDOM FOR GODLY LIVING

How often it occurs to me, as it must to you, that is far easier simply to cooperate with God!

Beth Moore

Be filled with the Holy Spirit; join a church where the members believe the Bible and know the Lord; seek the fellowship of other Christians; learn and be nourished by God's Word and His many promises. Conversion is not the end of your journey—it is only the beginning.

Corrie ten Boom

> *Then Jesus said to His disciples,*
> *"If anyone wants to come with Me,*
> *he must deny himself, take up his cross, and follow Me.*
> Matthew 16:24 Holman CSB

You cannot cooperate with Jesus in becoming what He wants you to become and simultaneously be what the world desires to make you. If you would say, "Take the world but give me Jesus," then you must deny yourself and take up your cross. The simple truth is that your "self" must be put to death in order for you to get to the point where for you to live is Christ. What will it be? The world and you, or Jesus and you? You do have a choice to make.

Kay Arthur

MORE WORDS FROM GOD'S WORD

And Jesus said unto them, Come ye after me, and I will make you to become fishers of men. And straightway they forsook their nets, and followed him.

Mark 1:17-18 KJV

He has showed you, O man, what is good. And what does the LORD require of you? To act justly and to love mercy and to walk humbly with your God.

Micah 6:8 NIV

If your life honors the name of Jesus, he will honor you.

2 Thessalonians 1:12 MSG

All of us who look forward to his Coming stay ready, with the glistening purity of Jesus' life as a model for our own.

1 John 3:3 MSG

My Priorities for Life

| | Check Your Priority | |
High	Med.	Low

I understand the importance of following Jesus.

| — | — | — |

For me, discipleship means obedience.

I believe that it is important for me to attempt to follow in Christ's footsteps, despite my imperfections.

| — | — | — |

| — | — | — |

Enthusiasm for Life

Whatever you do, do it enthusiastically,
as something done for the Lord and not for men.

Colossians 3:23 Holman CSB

Can you honestly say that you are an enthusiastic believer? Are you passionate about your faith and excited about your path? Hopefully so. But if your zest for life has waned, it is now time to redirect your efforts and recharge your spiritual batteries. And that means refocusing your values by putting God first.

Nothing is more important than your wholehearted commitment to your Creator and to His only begotten Son. Your faith must never be an afterthought; it must be your ultimate priority, your ultimate possession, and your ultimate passion. When you become passionate about your faith, you'll become passionate about your life, too.

Norman Vincent Peale advised, "Get absolutely enthralled with something. Throw yourself into it with abandon. Get out of yourself. Be somebody. Do something." His words still ring true. But sometimes, when the stresses of everyday life seem overwhelming, you may not feel very enthusiastic about your life or yourself. If so, it's time to reorder your thoughts, your priorities, your values, and your prayers. When you do, you'll be helping yourself, but you'll also be helping your family and friends.

Genuine, heartfelt, enthusiastic Christianity is contagious. If you enjoy a life-altering relationship with God, that relationship will have an impact on others—perhaps a profound impact.

Are you genuinely excited about your faith? And do you make your enthusiasm known to those around you? Or are you satisfied to be a "silent ambassador" for Christ? God's preference is clear: He intends that you stand before others and proclaim your faith.

Remember: You are the recipient of Christ's sacrificial love. Accept it enthusiastically and share it passionately. Jesus deserves your enthusiasm; the world deserves it; and you deserve the experience of sharing it.

Enthusiasm, like the flu, is contagious—
we get it from one another.

Barbara Johnson

PRIORITIES FOR MY LIFE

Don't wait for enthusiasm to find you . . . go looking for it. Look at you life and your relationships as exciting adventures. Don't wait for life to spice itself; spice things up yourself.

TIMELESS WISDOM FOR GODLY LIVING

One of the great needs in the church today is for every Christian to become enthusiastic about his faith in Jesus Christ.

Billy Graham

Each day, look for a kernel of excitement.

Barbara Jordan

Exuberance is beauty.

William Blake

Even if you live to be a hundred, never stop seeing the world through a child's eyes.

Marie T. Freeman

> *Never be lazy in your work,*
> *but serve the Lord enthusiastically.*
> *Romans 12:11 NLT*

What is required is sight and insight—then you might add one more: excite.

Robert Frost

MORE WORDS FROM GOD'S WORD

Whatever work you do, do your best, because you are going to the grave, where there is no working . . . .

Ecclesiastes 9:10 NCV

I have seen that there is nothing better than for a person to enjoy his activities, because that is his reward. For who can enable him to see what will happen after he dies?

Ecclesiastes 3:22 Holman CSB

Do your work with enthusiasm. Work as if you were serving the Lord, not as if you were serving only men and women.

Ephesians 6:7 NCV

He did it with all his heart. So he prospered.

2 Chronicles 31:21 NKJV

My Priorities for Life

My faith gives me reason to be enthusiastic about life.

	Check Your Priority	
High	Med.	Low
—	—	—

For me, it is important to generate enthusiastic thoughts and to associate with enthusiastic people.

—	—	—

When I praise God and thank Him for His blessings, I feel enthusiastic about life.

—	—	—

Courage for Everyday Living

Be strong and courageous, and do the work. Don't be afraid or discouraged by the size of the task, for the LORD God, my God, is with you. He will not fail you or forsake you.

1 Chronicles 28:20 NLT

Every life (including yours) is an unfolding series of events: some fabulous, some not-so-fabulous, and some downright disheartening. When you reach the mountaintops of life, praising God is easy. But, when the storm clouds form overhead, your faith will be tested, sometimes to the breaking point. As a believer, you can take comfort in this fact: Wherever you find yourself, whether at the top of the mountain or the depths of the valley, God is there, and because He cares for you, you can live courageously.

Believing Christians have every reason to be courageous. After all, the ultimate battle has already been fought and won on the cross at Calvary. But, even dedicated followers of Christ may find their courage tested by the inevitable disappointments and tragedies that occur in the lives of believers and non-believers alike.

The next time you find your courage tested to the limit, remember that God is as near as your next breath, and remember that He is your shield and your strength; He is your protector and your deliverer. Call upon Him in your hour of need and then be comforted. Whatever your challenge, whatever your trouble, God can handle it. And will.

If a person fears God, he or she has no reason to fear anything else. On the other hand, if a person does not fear God, then fear becomes a way of life.

Beth Moore

PRIORITIES FOR MY LIFE

Is your courage being tested? Cling tightly to God's promises, and pray. God can give you the strength to meet any challenge, and that's exactly what you should ask Him to do.

TIMELESS WISDOM FOR GODLY LIVING

With each new experience of letting God be in control, we gain courage and reinforcement for daring to do it again and again.

Gloria Gaither

When once we are assured that God is good, then there can be nothing left to fear.

Hannah Whitall Smith

What is courage? It is the ability to be strong in trust, in conviction, in obedience. To be courageous is to step out in faith— to trust and obey, no matter what.

Kay Arthur

God knows that the strength that comes from wrestling with our fear will give us wings to fly.

Paula Rinehart

> *Therefore, being always of good courage . . .*
> *we walk by faith, not by sight.*
> 2 Corinthians 5:6-7 NASB

God did away with all my fear. It was time for someone to stand up—or in my case, sit down. So I refused to move.

Rosa Parks

MORE WORDS FROM GOD'S WORD

The LORD himself goes before you and will be with you; he will never leave you nor forsake you. Do not be afraid; do not be discouraged.

Deuteronomy 31:8 NIV

But Moses said to the people, "Do not fear! Stand by and see the salvation of the LORD.

Exodus 14:13 NASB

In thee, O Lord, do I put my trust; let me never be put into confusion.

Psalm 71:1 KJV

My Priorities for Life

I understand the importance of living courageously.

I overcome fear by praying, and then by facing my fears head on.

I consider God to be my partner in every aspect of my life.

When I find myself in a situation that I cannot control, I turn my concerns over to God and leave the results up to Him.

Check Your Priority		
High	Med.	Low
—	—	—
—	—	—
—	—	—
—	—	—

Cheerful Christianity

Be cheerful. Keep things in good repair.
Keep your spirits up. Think in harmony. Be agreeable.
Do all that, and the God of love and peace will be with you for sure.

2 Corinthians 13:11 MSG

Cheerfulness is a gift that we give to others and to ourselves. And, as believers who have been saved by a risen Christ, why shouldn't we be cheerful? The answer, of course, is that we have every reason to honor our Savior with joy in our hearts, smiles on our faces, and words of celebration on our lips.

Few things in life are more sad, or, for that matter, more absurd, than the sight of grumpy Christians trudging unhappily through life. Christ promises us lives of abundance and joy if we accept His love and His grace. Yet sometimes, even the most righteous among us are beset by fits of ill temper and frustration. During these moments, we may not feel like turning our thoughts and prayers to Christ, but that's precisely what we should do.

John Wesley correctly observed, "Sour godliness is the devil's religion." These words remind us that pessimism and doubt are some of the most important tools that Satan uses to achieve his objectives. Our challenge, of course, is to ensure that Satan cannot use these tools on us.

Are you a cheerful Christian? You should be! And what is the best way to attain the joy that is rightfully yours? By giving Christ what is rightfully His: your heart, your soul, and your life.

Cheerfulness prepares a glorious mind for all the noblest acts of religion—love, adoration, praise, and every union with our God.

St. Elizabeth Ann Seton

Is anyone happy? Let him sing songs of praise.

James 5:13 NIV

PRIORITIES FOR MY LIFE

Do you need a little cheering up? If so, find somebody else who needs cheering up, too. Then, do your best to brighten that person's day. When you do, you'll discover that cheering up other people is a wonderful way to cheer yourself up, too!

TIMELESS WISDOM FOR GODLY LIVING

The greatest honor you can give Almighty God is to live gladly and joyfully because of the knowledge of His love.

Juliana of Norwich

God is good, and heaven is forever. And if those two facts don't cheer you up, nothing will.

Marie T. Freeman

We may run, walk, stumble, drive, or fly, but let us never lose sight of the reason for the journey, or miss a chance to see a rainbow on the way.

Gloria Gaither

When we bring sunshine into the lives of others, we're warmed by it ourselves. When we spill a little happiness, it splashes on us.

Barbara Johnson

God loves a cheerful giver.
2 Corinthians 9:7 NIV

Make each day useful and cheerful and prove that you know the worth of time by employing it well. Then youth will be happy, old age without regret, and life a beautiful success.

Louisa May Alcott

MORE WORDS FROM GOD'S WORD

A cheerful look brings joy to the heart, and good news gives health to the bones.

Proverbs 15:30 NIV

Do everything readily and cheerfully—no bickering, no second-guessing allowed! Go out into the world uncorrupted, a breath of fresh air in this squalid and polluted society. Provide people with a glimpse of good living and of the living God. Carry the light-giving Message into the night.

Philippians 2:14-15 MSG

Jacob said, "For what a relief it is to see your friendly smile. It is like seeing the smile of God!"

Genesis 33:10 NLT

My Priorities for Life

	Check Your Priority	
High	Med.	Low

For me, it is important to cultivate an attitude of cheerfulness.

— — —

I believe that happiness is not a goal. Happiness is the by-product of my right relationship with God.

— — —

Because I understand that emotions are contagious, I try my best to associate with cheerful people.

— — —

You Can Count on Him

Whatever God has promised gets stamped with the Yes of Jesus.
In him, this is what we preach and pray, the great Amen,
God's Yes and our Yes together, gloriously evident.

2 Corinthians 1:20 MSG

What do you expect from the day ahead? Are you expecting God to do wonderful things, or are you living beneath a cloud of apprehension and doubt? The familiar words of Psalm 118:24 remind us of a profound yet simple truth: "This is the day which the LORD hath made; we will rejoice and be glad in it" (KJV).

For Christian believers, every day begins and ends with God's Son and God's promises. When we accept Christ into our hearts, God promises us the opportunity for earthy peace and spiritual abundance. But more importantly, God promises us the priceless gift of eternal life.

As we face the inevitable challenges of life-here-on-earth, we must arm ourselves with the promises of God's Holy Word. When we do, we can expect the best, not only for the day ahead, but also for all eternity.

We have ample evidence that the Lord is able to guide.
The promises cover every imaginable situation.
All we need to do is to take the hand he stretches out.

Elisabeth Elliot

*When God wanted to guarantee his promises, he gave his word,
a rock-solid guarantee. God can't break his word.
And because his word cannot change, the promise is likewise
unchangeable. It's an unbreakable spiritual lifeline, reaching past
all appearances right to the very presence of God.*

Hebrews 6:17-19 MSG

PRIORITIES FOR MY LIFE

Do you really trust God's promises, or are you hedging your
bets? Today, think about the role that God's Word plays in your
life, and think about ways that you can worry less and trust God
more.

TIMELESS WISDOM FOR GODLY LIVING

The meaning of hope isn't just some flimsy wishing. It's a firm confidence in God's promises—that he will ultimately set things right.

Sheila Walsh

Fear and doubt are conquered by a faith that rejoices. And faith can rejoice because the promises of God are as certain as God Himself.

Kay Arthur

Gather the riches of God's promises which can strengthen you in the time when there will be no freedom.

Corrie ten Boom

Let us hold fast the confession of our hope without wavering, for He who promised is faithful.
Hebrews 10:23 NASB

When we meditate on God and remember the promises He has given us in His Word, our faith grows, and our fears dissolve.

Charles Stanley

MORE WORDS FROM GOD'S WORD

And we desire that each one of you show the same diligence so as to realize the full assurance of hope until the end, so that you will not be sluggish, but imitators of those who through faith and patience inherit the promises.

Hebrews 6:11-12 NASB

As for God, his way is perfect. All the LORD's promises prove true. He is a shield for all who look to him for protection.

Psalm 18:30 NLT

This is my comfort in my affliction: Your promise has given me life.

Psalm 119:50 Holman CSB

My Priorities for Life

I believe God's promises, and I am willing to base my life on those promises.

I trust that God keeps His promises to me, and I will strive to keep my promises to Him.

Because I should remain mindful of God's promises, I continue to study God's Word.

Check Your Priority		
High	Med.	Low
—	—	—
—	—	—
—	—	—

Using Your Talents

*God has given gifts to each of you from his
great variety of spiritual gifts.
Manage them well so that God's generosity can flow through you.*

1 Peter 4:10 NLT

God has given you an array of talents, and He has given you unique opportunities to share those talents with the world. Your Creator intends for you to use your talents for the glory of His kingdom in the service of His children. Will you honor Him by sharing His gifts? And, will you share His gifts humbly and lovingly? Hopefully you will.

As a woman who has been touched by the transforming love of Jesus Christ, your obligation is clear: You must strive to make the most of your own God-given talents, and you must encourage your family and friends to do likewise.

Today, make this promise to yourself and to God: Promise to use your talents to minister to your family, to your friends, and to the world. And remember: The best way to say "Thank You" for God's gifts is to use them.

When I stand before God at the end of my life,
I would hope that I would not have a single bit of talent left
and could say, "I used everything you gave me."

Erma Bombeck

According to the grace given to us, we have different gifts:
If prophecy, use it according to the standard of faith; if service,
in service; if teaching, in teaching; if exhorting, in exhortation;
giving, with generosity; leading, with diligence;
showing mercy, with cheerfulness.

Romans 12:6-8 Holman CSB

PRIORITIES FOR MY LIFE

Converting talent into skill requires work. Remember the old adage: "What we are is God's gift to us; what we become is our gift to God."

TIMELESS WISDOM FOR GODLY LIVING

Not everyone possesses boundless energy or a conspicuous talent. We are not equally blessed with great intellect or physical beauty or emotional strength. But we have all been given the same ability to be faithful.

Gigi Graham Tchividjian

Life is not easy for any of us. But what of that? We must have perseverance and above all confidence in ourselves. We must believe that we are gifted for something and that this thing must be attained.

Marie Curie

God gives talent. Work transforms talent into genius.

Anna Pavlova

Do not neglect the gift that is in you.
1 Timothy 4:14 Holman CSB

Whether we are poets or parents or teachers or artists or gardeners, we must start where we are and use what we have. In the process of creation and relationship, what seems mundane and trivial may show itself to be holy, precious, part of a pattern.

Luci Shaw

MORE WORDS FROM GOD'S WORD

I remind you to fan into flame the gift of God.

2 Timothy 1:6 NIV

There are different kinds of gifts, but they are all from the same Spirit. There are different ways to serve but the same Lord to serve.

1 Corinthians 12:4–5 NCV

His master said to him, "Well done, good and faithful slave! You were faithful over a few things; I will put you in charge of many things. Enter your master's joy!"

Matthew 25:21 Holman CSB

Every good gift and every perfect gift is from above, and cometh down from the Father of lights.

James 1:17 KJV

My Priorities for Life

I believe that God wants me to take risks to do the work that He intends for me to do.

I believe that it is important to associate with people who encourage me to use my talents.

I believe that it is important to honor God by using the talents He has given me.

Check Your Priority		
High	Med.	Low
—	—	—
—	—	—
—	—	—

When Mistakes Happen

Therefore, if anyone is in Christ, he is a new creation;
the old has gone, the new has come!

2 Corinthians 5:17 NIV

Everybody makes mistakes, and so will you. In fact, you should expect to make mistakes—plenty of mistakes—but you should not allow those missteps to rob you of the enthusiasm you need to fulfill God's plan for your life.

We are imperfect people living in an imperfect world; mistakes are simply part of the price we pay for being here. But, even though mistakes are an inevitable part of life's journey, repeated mistakes should not be. When we commit the inevitable blunders of life, we must correct them, learn from them, and pray for the wisdom not to repeat them. When we do, our mistakes become lessons, and our lives become adventures in growth, not stagnation.

When our shortcomings are made public, we may feel embarrassed or worse. We may presume (quite incorrectly) that "everybody" is concerned with the gravity of our problem. And, as a consequence, we may feel the need to hide from our problems rather than confront them. To do so is wrong. Even when our pride is bruised, we must face up to our mistakes and seek to rise above them.

Have you made a king-sized blunder or two? Of course you have. But here's the big question: have you used your mistakes as stumbling blocks or stepping stones? The answer to this question will determine how well you perform in the workplace and in every other aspect of your life. So don't let the fear of past failures hold you back. And remember this: Even if you've made a colossal mistake, God isn't finished with you yet—in fact, He's probably just getting started.

Mistakes offer the possibility for redemption
and a new start in God's kingdom.
No matter what you're guilty of,
God can restore your innocence.

Barbara Johnson

PRIORITIES FOR MY LIFE

Made a mistake? Ask for forgiveness! If you've broken one of God's rules, you can always ask Him for His forgiveness. And He will always give it!

TIMELESS WISDOM FOR GODLY LIVING

Mature people are not emotionally and spiritually devastated by every mistake they make. They are able to maintain some kind of balance in their lives.

Joyce Meyer

When we focus on God, the scene changes. He's in control of our lives; nothing lies outside the realm of His redemptive grace. Even when we make mistakes, fail in relationships, or deliberately make bad choices, God can redeem us.

Penelope J. Stokes

Lord, when we are wrong, make us willing to change; and when we are right, make us easy to live with.

Peter Marshall

If we confess our sins to him, he is faithful and just to forgive us and to cleanse us from every wrong.
1 John 1:9 NLT

We become a failure when we allow mistakes to take away our ability to learn, give, grow, and try again.

Susan Lenzkes

MORE WORDS FROM GOD'S WORD

Have mercy on me, O God, according to your unfailing love; according to your great compassion blot out my transgressions. Wash away all my iniquity and cleanse me from my sin.

Psalm 51:1-2 NIV

You were taught, with regard to your former way of life, to put off your old self, which is being corrupted by its deceitful desires; to be made new in the attitude of your minds; and to put on the new self, created to be like God in true righteousness and holiness.

Ephesians 4:22-24 NIV

Have mercy on me, O God, according to your unfailing love; according to your great compassion blot out my transgressions. Wash away all my iniquity and cleanse me from my sin.

Psalm 51:1-2 NIV

My Priorities for Life

I believe that it is important to examine my mistakes in order to improve my work.

I know when I make a mistake, the time to make things better is now, not later!

I understand that a mistake is never permanent (unless I do nothing to fix it).

Check Your Priority		
High	Med.	Low
—	—	—
—	—	—
—	—	—

Celebrating Life

Celebrate God all day, every day. I mean, revel in him!

Philippians 4:4 MSG

D o you celebrate the gifts God has given you? Do you pray without ceasing? Do you rejoice in the beauty of God's glorious creation? You should. But perhaps, as a busy woman living in a demanding world, you have been slow to count your gifts and even slower to give thanks to the Giver.

As God's children, we are all blessed beyond measure, and we should celebrate His blessings every day that we live. The gifts we receive from God are multiplied when we share them with others. Today is a non-renewable resource—once it's gone, it's gone forever. Our responsibility—as believers—is to give thanks for God's gifts and then use them in the service of God's will and in the service of His people.

God has blessed us beyond measure, and we owe Him everything, including our praise. And let us remember that for those of us who have been saved by God's only begotten Son, every day is a cause for celebration.

If you can forgive the person you were, accept the person you are,
and believe in the person you will become,
you are headed for joy. So celebrate your life.

Barbara Johnson

Not every day of our lives is overflowing with joy and celebration.
But there are moments when our hearts nearly burst within us
for the sheer joy of being alive. The first sight of our newborn
babies, the warmth of love in another's eyes, the fresh scent of
rain on a hot summer's eve—moments like these renew
in us a heartfelt appreciation for life.

Gwen Ellis

PRIORITIES FOR MY LIFE

While you're celebrating life, don't try and keep the celebration
to yourself. Let other people know why you're rejoicing, and
don't be bashful about telling them how they can rejoice, too.

TIMELESS WISDOM FOR GODLY LIVING

All our life is a celebration for us; we are convinced, in fact, that God is always everywhere. We sing while we work . . . we pray while we carry out all life's other occupations.

St. Clement of Alexandria

I am truly happy with Jesus Christ. I couldn't live without Him.

Ruth Bell Graham

Christ is the secret, the source, the substance, the center, and the circumference of all true and lasting gladness.

Mrs. Charles E. Cowman

David and the whole house of Israel were celebrating with all their might before the LORD, with songs and with harps, lyres, tambourines, sistrums and cymbals.
2 Samuel 6:5 NIV

A joyful heart is like a sunshine of God's love, the hope of eternal happiness, a burning flame of God . . . . And if we pray, we will become that sunshine of God's love—in our own home, the place where we live, and in the world at large.

Mother Teresa

MORE WORDS FROM GOD'S WORD

At the dedication of the wall of Jerusalem, the Levites were sought out from where they lived and were brought to Jerusalem to celebrate joyfully the dedication with songs of thanksgiving and with the music of cymbals, harps and lyres.

Nehemiah 12:27 NIV

A happy heart is like a continual feast.

Proverbs 15:15 NCV

Shout for joy to the LORD, all the earth. Worship the LORD with gladness; come before him with joyful songs.

Psalm 100:1-2 NIV

So now we can rejoice in our wonderful new relationship with God—all because of what our Lord Jesus Christ has done for us in making us friends of God.

Romans 5:11 NLT

My Priorities for Life

	Check Your Priority	
High	Med.	Low

I understand the need to celebrate God's gifts.

— — —

I will celebrate God's gifts with my family and friends.

— — —

I will consider each new day a cause for celebration.

— — —

Decisions, Decisions, Decisions

If you don't know what you're doing, pray to the Father.
He loves to help. You'll get his help, and won't be condescended to
when you ask for it. Ask boldly, believingly, without a second thought.
People who "worry their prayers" are like wind-whipped waves.
Don't think you're going to get anything from the Master that way,
adrift at sea, keeping all your options open.

James 1:5-8 MSG

Life is a series of choices. From the instant we wake in the morning until the moment we nod off to sleep at night, we make countless decisions: decisions about the things we do, decisions about the words we speak, and decisions about the thoughts we choose to think. Simply put, the quality of those decisions determines the quality of our lives.

Some decisions are easy to make because the consequences of those decisions are small. When the person behind the counter asks, "Want fries with that?" the necessary response requires little thought because the consequences of that decision are minor.

Some decisions, on the other hand, are big . . . very big. The biggest decision, of course, is one that far too many people ignore: the decision concerning God's only begotten Son. But if you're a believer in Christ, you've already made that choice, and you have received God's gift of grace. Perhaps now you're asking yourself "What's next, Lord?" If so, you may be facing a series of big decisions concerning your life and your future. Here are some things you can do: 1. Gather as much information as you can: don't expect to get all the facts—that's impossible—but get as many facts as you can in a reasonable amount of time. (Proverbs 24:3-4) 2. Don't be too impulsive: If you have time to make a decision, use that time to make a good decision. (Proverbs 19:2) 3. Rely on the advice of trusted friends and mentors. Proverbs 1:5 makes it clear: "A wise man will hear and increase learning, and a man of understanding will attain wise counsel." (NKJV) 4. Pray for guidance. When you seek it, He will give it. (Luke 11:9) 5. Trust the quiet inner voice of your conscience: Treat your conscience as you would a trusted advisor. (Luke 17:21) 6. When the time for action arrives, act. Procrastination is the enemy of progress; don't let it defeat you. (James 1:22)

When we learn to listen to Christ's voice for the details of our daily decisions, we begin to know Him personally.

Catherine Marshall

PRIORITIES FOR MY LIFE

As you make decisions throughout the day, consult God in prayer, even if those prayers are brief.

TIMELESS WISDOM FOR GODLY LIVING

There may be no trumpet sound or loud applause when we make a right decision, just a calm sense of resolution and peace.

Gloria Gaither

No trumpets sound when the important decisions of our lives are made. Destiny is made known silently.

Agnes DeMille

If you are struggling to make some difficult decisions right now that aren't specifically addressed in the Bible, don't make a choice based on what's right for someone else. You are the Lord's and He will make sure you do what's right.

Lisa Whelchel

The principle of making no decision without prayer keeps me from rushing in and committing myself before I consult God.

Elizabeth George

Ignorant zeal is worthless; haste makes waste.
Proverbs 19:2 MSG

The location of your affections will drive the direction of your decisions.

Lisa Bevere

MORE WORDS FROM GOD'S WORD

But Daniel purposed in his heart that he would not defile himself....

Daniel 1:8 KJV

I am offering you life or death, blessings or curses. Now, choose life! . . . To choose life is to love the Lord your God, obey him, and stay close to him.

Deuteronomy 30:19-20 NCV

The thing you should want most is God's kingdom and doing what God wants. Then all these other things you need will be given to you.

Matthew 6:33 NCV

Above all and before all, do this: Get Wisdom! Write this at the top of your list: Get Understanding!

Proverbs 4:7 MSG

My Priorities for Life

I understand the importance of making decisions based upon the teachings of God's Word.

In making important decisions, I understand the importance of seeking God's guidance.

I understand that I am accountable for the decisions I make.

Check Your Priority		
High	Med.	Low
—	—	—
—	—	—
—	—	—

Accepting God's Forgiveness

Be even-tempered, content with second place, quick to forgive an offense.
Forgive as quickly and completely as the Master forgave you.
And regardless of what else you put on, wear love. It's your basic,
all-purpose garment. Never be without it.

Colossians 3:13-14 MSG

All of us have sinned. Sometimes our sins result from our own stubborn rebellion against God's commandments. Sometimes, we are swept up by events that encourage us to behave in ways that we later come to regret. And sometimes, even when our intentions are honorable, we make mistakes that have long-lasting consequences. When we look back at our actions with remorse, we may experience intense feelings of guilt. But God has an answer for the guilt that we feel. That answer, of course, is His forgiveness.

When we genuinely repent from our wrongdoings, and when we sincerely confess our sins, we are forgiven by our Heavenly Father. But long after God has forgiven us, we may continue to withhold forgiveness from ourselves. Instead of accepting God's mercy and accepting our past, we may think long and hard—far too long and hard—about the things that "might have been," the things that "could have been," or the things that "should have been."

Are you troubled by feelings of guilt, even after you've received God's forgiveness? Are you still struggling with painful memories of mistakes you made long ago? Are you focused so intently on yesterday that your vision of today is clouded? If so you still have work to do—spiritual work. You should ask your Heavenly Father not for forgiveness (He granted that gift the very first time you asked Him!) but instead for acceptance and trust: acceptance of the past and trust in God's plan for your life.

Once you have asked God for His forgiveness, you can be certain that your Heavenly Father has given it. And if He, in His infinite wisdom, will forgive your sins, how then can you withhold forgiveness from yourself? The answer, of course, is that once God has forgiven you, you should forgive yourself, too.

When you forgive yourself thoroughly and completely, you'll stop investing energy in those most useless of emotions: bitterness, regret, and self-recrimination. And you can then get busy making the world a better place, and that's as it should be. After all, since God has forgiven you, isn't it about time that you demonstrate your gratitude by serving Him?

PRIORITIES FOR MY LIFE

If you've asked for God's forgiveness, He has given it. But have you forgiven yourself? If not, the best moment to do so is this one.

TIMELESS WISDOM FOR GODLY LIVING

I believe that forgiveness can become a continuing cycle: because God forgives us, we're to forgive others; because we forgive others, God forgives us. Scripture presents both parts of the cycle.

Shirley Dobson

Have you thought that your willingness to forgive is really your affirmation of the power of God to do you good?

Paula Rinehart

God has been very gracious to me, for I never dwell upon anything wrong which a person has done to me, as to remember it afterwards. If I do remember it, I always see some other virtue in the person.

St. Teresa of Avila

Hatred stirs up trouble, but love forgives all wrongs.
Proverbs 10:12 NCV

Forgiveness is actually the best revenge because it not only sets us free from the person we forgive, but it frees us to move into all that God has in store for us.

Stormie Omartian

MORE WORDS FROM GOD'S WORD

Our Father is kind; you be kind. "Don't pick on people, jump on their failures, criticize their faults—unless, of course, you want the same treatment. Don't condemn those who are down; that hardness can boomerang. Be easy on people; you'll find life a lot easier.

Luke 6:36-37 MSG

Be gentle with one another, sensitive. Forgive one another as quickly and thoroughly as God in Christ forgave you.

Ephesians 4:32 MSG

Whenever you stand praying, forgive, if you have anything against anyone, so that your Father in heaven will also forgive you your transgressions.

Mark 11:25 NASB

Praise the Lord, I tell myself, and never forget the good things he does for me. He forgives all my sins and heals all my diseases.

Psalm 103:3 NLT

My Priorities for Life

	Check Your Priority		
	High	Med.	Low
I understand that when I ask God for forgiveness, He grants it.	—	—	—
Because God has forgiven me, I can forgive others.	—	—	—
Because God has forgiven me, I can forgive myself.	—	—	—

Considering the Cross

For Christ did not send me to baptize, but to preach the gospel—
not with clever words, so that the cross of Christ
will not be emptied of its effect.

1 Corinthians 1:17 Holman CSB

On a Friday morning, on a hill at Calvary, Jesus was crucified. Darkness came over the land, the curtain of the temple was torn in two, and finally Jesus called out, "Father, into your hands I commit my spirit" (Luke 23:46 NIV). Christ had endured the crucifixion, and it was finished.

The body of Jesus was wrapped in a linen shroud and placed in a new tomb. It was there that God breathed life into His Son. It was there that Christ was resurrected. It was there that the angels rejoiced. And it was there, that God's plan for the salvation of mankind was made complete.

As we consider Christ's sacrifice on the cross, we should be profoundly humbled and profoundly grateful. And today, as we come to Christ in prayer, we should do so in a spirit of quiet, heartfelt devotion to the One who gave His life so that we might have life eternal.

Christ suffered on the cross for you. He shed His blood—for you. He has offered to walk with you through this life and throughout all eternity. As you approach Him today in prayer, think about His sacrifice and His love. And be humble.

To view ourselves through our Creator's loving, tear-filled eyes,
we need to climb Calvary's hill and look down from
the cross of Christ—for that is where God declared that we
are worth the life of His precious Son.

Susan Lenzkes

Keep your eyes on Jesus, who both began and finished this race we're in.
Study how he did it. Because he never lost sight of where he was headed,
that exhilarating finish in and with God, he could put up
with anything along the way: cross, shame, whatever.
And now he's there, in the place of honor, right alongside God.

Hebrews 12:2 MSG

PRIORITIES FOR MY LIFE

At the foot of the cross, believers gain perspective: Rebecca
Manley Pippert writes, "Dust, rusty nails, and blood
notwithstanding, the ground at the foot of the cross is the only
vantage point from which to view life clearly. To see things there
is to see them truly."

TIMELESS WISDOM FOR GODLY LIVING

The cross takes care of the past. The cross takes care of the flesh.
The cross takes care of the world.

Kay Arthur

Tell me the story of Jesus. Write on my heart every word. Tell me
the story most precious, sweetest that ever was heard.

Fanny Crosby

God is my heavenly Father. He loves me with an everlasting love.
The proof of that is the Cross.

Elisabeth Elliot

*This Jesus, following the deliberate and well-thought-out plan
of God, was betrayed by men who took the law into their own
hands, and was handed over to you. And you pinned him to
a cross and killed him. But God untied the death ropes and
raised him up. Death was no match for him.*

Acts 2:23-24 MSG

Jesus came down from heaven, revealing exactly what God is like,
offering eternal life and a personal relationship with God, on the
condition of our rebirth—a rebirth made possible through His
own death on the cross.

Anne Graham Lotz

MORE WORDS FROM GOD'S WORD

But as for me, I will never boast about anything except the cross of our Lord Jesus Christ, through whom the world has been crucified to me, and I to the world.

Galatians 6:14 Holman CSB

Then they spat in His face and beat Him; and others struck Him with the palms of their hands.

Matthew 26:67 NKJV

Then He said to them all, "If anyone wants to come with Me, he must deny himself, take up his cross daily, and follow Me."

Luke 9:23 Holman CSB

And being found in appearance as a man, he humbled himself and became obedient to death—even death on a cross!

Philippians 2:8 NIV

My Priorities for Life

I accept the loving act of Jesus on the cross as my way to salvation.

I am thankful for the loving gift of my Heavenly Father: the sacrificial gift of His Son, Jesus.

I bear my own cross by being obedient to Jesus.

Check Your Priority		
High	Med.	Low
—	—	—
—	—	—
—	—	—

— 313 —

The thing you should want most is
God's kingdom and doing what God wants.
Then all these other things you need
will be given to you.

Matthew 6:33 NCV

TOPIC	TITLE	PAGE